Endorsements

Few people understand the Bible from an exegetical and practical perspective as does Ken Hemphill. As a pastor, seminary president, and denominational leader, he has maintained a constant study of God's Word. His extensive, published works flow from his study of the Bible. From constantly interacting with church members, students, and others, Dr. Hemphill knows how to relate Bible study to the average person and to the scholar. His work, *Mining for Gold*, will benefit readers from every walk of life. I look forward to using this book in my classes at MABTS and in my personal study.

> —**Jere Phillips, PhD**, professor of Practical Theology
> and editor, *The Journal of Mid-America Baptist
> Theological Seminary*

Ken Hemphill has given the church a much needed resource in his book *Mining for Gold*. Well written, thorough, and easily understood, this book can be used in multiple ways. Given the post-Christian culture of our day, these basic tools for understanding biblical truths and doctrines are most timely and very effective.

> —**Susie Hawkins**, author and Bible study teacher

Finally, there is an inspiring and practical book to help others get the most from their study of God's Word. I recommend *Mining for Gold* to new and experienced Christians who want to know God more intimately.

> —**Daryl Eldridge, PhD**, president and cofounder of
> Rockbridge Seminary

Thank God for profound forays into the nature and purpose of Scripture, but what is needed is a book for the church. Dr. Ken Hemphill is forever looking to assist the church of God. *Mining for Gold* is a book informed by scholarly endeavor, yet cogent for every church member with a desire for God's Word. At this time in the American sojourn, my prayer for the church is that she will rediscover the gold to be mined in the Bible. This book is the path that will lead to those mines.

—**Dr. Paige Patterson**, president of Southwestern Baptist Theological Seminary

Practical! This was the first word that came to my mind as I read *Mining for Gold*. My friend, Ken Hemphill, has provided the church with a resource that moves in-depth Bible study out of the pulpit and into the pews. I believe this book will energize and equip Christians to get more out of their personal time in God's Word.

—**Ryan Pack**, senior pastor, First Baptist Church of North Augusta, SC

Each morning every Christian should read the Bible to hear the voice of God and then pray its promises back to the Lord. In his latest book, *Mining for Gold*, Dr. Ken Hemphill has given us an excellent tool to teach us how to dig into God's Word to discover the priceless jewels of His promises so we can live in faith and walk in victory. I highly recommend this practical book.

—**Steve Gaines, PhD**, senior pastor, Bellevue Baptist Church in Memphis, TN and president, Southern Baptist Convention

Mining for Gold not only teaches Christians how to study the Bible, it puts a fire in their souls to study God's Word! This book has something for everyone, from new Christians to seminary students.

—**Steve Scoggins**, senior pastor, First Baptist Church of Hendersonville, NC

According to Ezra we are to "prepare our hearts to study, do, and teach the Word." In *Mining for Gold*, Dr. Hemphill helps us learn how to mine the nuggets of gold in God's Word in order to obey His instructions.

—**Johnny M. Hunt**, senior pastor, First Baptist Church of Woodstock, Georgia

I am so thankful that in the early years of my faith walk I had a pastor who admonished me to study God's Word for myself. He was adamant that I needed to know the Word so I would know truth and never allow it to be distorted. Ken Hemphill has spent his life in the Word, and it is so exciting to know that God has laid on his heart the desire to teach others how to learn truth and discern His will. Dr. Hemphill has done the church a great favor by providing this simple to use book that will help readers to accurately handle the word of truth (2 Tim. 2:15).

—**Sheila West**, director of administration, Heritage Community Church in Fruitland Park, FL

Mining for Gold is a book that I wish would be read by every Christian in America. Dr. Ken Hemphill—long recognized as an expert on church growth, church health, and the rightful application of God's Word—clearly explains what it means to let Scripture impact and shape our lives. Hemphill lays out a call that can't be ignored—a challenge to follow the Lord without compromise, and he gives the tools to help readers understand how the timeless truths of the Bible relate to our world today.

—**Alex McFarland**, director, The Center for Apologetics and Christian Worldview, North Greenville University

I'm grateful for leaders during my formative years who taught me the importance of studying, memorizing, and obeying the Bible. But I'm afraid in today's church culture an emphasis on personal experience has often replaced biblical discipleship, resulting in a weaker, shallow, and emotionally driven church. I'm thankful that Dr. Hemphill's work calls a new generation of Christians to the eternal treasure of God's written Word, encouraging them to "mine for gold." *Mining for Gold* is a valuable tool that brings us back to the strong, biblical foundation of our faith!

> —**Dr. Larry Steven McDonald**, professor of Christian Spirituality; dean, Graduate School of Christian Ministry; and, director, Doctor of Ministry Studies, North Greenville University

Students of the Bible always hunt for new and improved ways to study the Scriptures. Ken Hemphill accomplishes that task by putting in the hands of Bible readers a resource to mine the best out of Bible reading and study. I'm recommending this book to our church. Read and rejoice!

> —**Ralph Douglas West**, senior pastor, The Church Without Walls in Houston, Texas

The prophet Jeremiah said that if a person is to be purposefully successful they need to understand and know the Lord. In *Mining for Gold*, Dr. Hemphill gives to the Christ-follower the basic tools for reading, studying, and understanding the ways of God revealed through His Word. Instead of capitulating to the latest church culture trend, church leaders must be serious about equipping devoted, reproducing disciples. *Mining for Gold* is one of those simple, concise, yet amazing resources to facilitate a biblically based equipping model for the local church with a desire to be faithful Christ-followers.

> —**Dr. John Yeats**, executive director, Missouri Baptist Convention and recording secretary, Southern Baptist Convention

Dr. Ken Hemphill has done a great service for believers young and old by writing this book on Bible study. As he taught the basis of this study to our church, it created a new thirst for God's Word among our people. Because there is such a lack of practical guidelines available today for believers who need to increase their Bible knowledge, *Mining for Gold* is a much-needed resource for the church.

—**Dr. Paul Fleming**, executive pastor, Forestville Baptist Church in Greenville, SC

A great need exists in the church today for equipping members to read and understand the Bible for themselves. Most books on studying the Bible are written for pastors. Ken Hemphill brings practical resources together to help every church member. In *Mining for Gold* you will learn how to dig into the rich treasure that is the Word of God.

—**Kenneth Priest**, director of Convention Strategies, Southern Baptists of Texas Convention

To reach people far from God in an increasingly post-Christian culture, our church is continually looking for resources that will help us make disciples. *Mining for Gold* is a valuable resource for the church to help believers discover the treasure of God's Word. Dr. Ken Hemphill has written this book out of the wealth of his experience as pastor and theological educator, making the sometime complex issues involved in interpreting Scripture accessible to followers of Jesus who have just begun their journey of faith as well as for those who have walked with Jesus for years.

—**Eric Thomas**, senior pastor, First Baptist Church of Norfolk, VA

The importance of careful and accurate interpretation of the Bible was recognized by the Scriptures themselves—"Be diligent . . . accurately handling the word of truth" (2 Tim. 2:15). Dr. Hemphill has offered a very helpful and accessible study that allows us to respond to the biblical mandate to accurately handle the Word of the Lord by learning to better interpret it, in order to properly apply the Word to present-day issues and living. With *Mining for Gold*, one does not need to become a biblical scholar in order to effectively interpret the Bible.

> —**Randall J. Pannell, PhD**, interim president and chief academic officer, North Greenville University

Ken Hemphill knows the Word of God and preaches it clearly and with conviction. His suggestions on how to read and study the Bible are priceless and worth the "gold" you will pay for the book. Studying the Bible is not new. My good friend, Ken, has written the timeless principles of studying the Bible and presents them in a unique and new way. Read to study the Bible, and then read it to grow.

> —**Elmer L. Towns**, cofounder and vice president of Liberty University

MINING
FOR
GOLD

MINING
FOR
GOLD

DISCOVERING GOD'S
TRUTH FOR YOURSELF

KEN HEMPHILL

Auxano
PRESS

To
Sloane Elizabeth Banks,
my granddaughter,
an active and adventurous young lady who
lives each day with enthusiasm.
May God give you fullness of life as
you discover His truth through the study of His Word!

Contents

Acknowledgments

My passion is to know and obey God's Word. I have profited greatly by sitting at the feet of great Bible teachers, beginning with my dad, Carl Hemphill, who was my pastor throughout my early childhood. My dad instilled in me a love for God's Word and a desire to understand it fully. Thus he also taught me how to study the Bible for myself. He wanted me to develop biblical convictions that were my own.

I learned much about the Bible through Sunday school teachers and adults who mentored me through summer studies in Vacation Bible School. Many of these rudimentary Bible study skills were enhanced greatly through my studies at various seminaries. I have since had the opportunity to teach at several seminaries and have had the joy of helping countless students learn how to study the Bible for themselves.

Recently I was privileged to be the interim pastor at Forestville Baptist Church in Travelers Rest, South Carolina. My good friend and associate pastor, Paul Fleming, invited me to teach a few extra sessions on "How to Study the Bible for Yourself." The response to those three simple lessons led to the writing and publication of this book.

Paula, my wife and ministry companion of many years, has always shared my joy for Bible study and teaching. She continues to inspire me to excellence in ministry.

My children and grandchildren are always in mind as I write. Kristina, my oldest, and her husband Brett, are involved in mission ministry. Both are accomplished Bible students, and Kristina is an accomplished writer. Rachael has been involved in children's ministry in the local church and has also worked with Rethink, an organization that writes children's curriculum. She now serves faithfully as a layperson, encouraging effective children's ministry in her local church. Katie and Daniel are both students of the Word and are actively involved in their church in Germantown, Tennessee. My ten grandchildren are my delight, and I have written this book with them in mind. I want them to develop a great love for and understanding of God's Word so they can discover His truth for their own lives. A few years ago, I began the process of dedicating my books to my grandchildren, beginning with the oldest. This one is dedicated to one of Katie's and Daniel's daughters.

I am thankful to Auxano Press for publishing and promoting this book. The goal of Auxano Press is to provide biblically sound and reasonably priced tools to help individuals and churches experience balanced growth.

I am grateful for the partnership Auxano formed with Bookmasters for the broader distribution of Auxano products.

I am indebted to Jody Jennings and Frankie Melton, colleagues at North Greenville University, who gave valuable input early in the process. North Greenville has allowed me to continue my ministry to local churches through the Center for Church Planting and Revitalization. Many of the books published through Auxano Press are part of our revitalization process. We believe that nothing changes the heart and mind but the Word of God applied by His Spirit.

I am grateful to my good friend, John Hughes, who also provided helpful suggestions about tools for Bible study.

I must also thank Maleah Bell for her editing work, which greatly enhanced the manuscript I provided to her.

Finally, I have profited greatly from reading numerous books on studying the Bible, and several have been footnoted where I have borrowed from the ideas of great men who have come before me. For these authors and their work I am grateful.

Preface

As a young pastor in Norfolk, Virginia, I taught new member's classes. The purpose of the classes was to give our new members an overview of our church, our doctrinal commitment, and the importance of personal and corporate Bible study. One young lady, a recent convert, sat through the Bible study portion of a particular class with her brand new Bible closed on the table in front of her. I first thought that she may have been embarrassed to use her Bible because she was unfamiliar with the books of the Bible and thus was afraid she might not be able to find a particular text. I took a moment to go over the divisions of the Bible and the order of the books with the entire class. I showed them the table of contents in the front and paid special attention to the book we were studying. Still, she made no movement toward her Bible! After the class, I asked her privately why she had not opened her Bible to follow our study. She timidly explained that she had grown up in a tradition where only the priest was qualified to understand and teach the Bible, and therefore she felt unworthy and unqualified to open the Bible.

I tended to be a Bible teacher from the pulpit, and therefore it was common for a majority of the congregation to have their Bibles and notebooks open while I was preaching. This was true even for the choir who sat in an open choir loft behind the pulpit. During a certain season of my ministry in Norfolk, a number of search committees from other churches visited our church to see if I might be open to being their pastor. One particular committee, who visited for several weeks in a row, remarked that they were most impressed to see so many people, even choir members, with their Bibles open in their laps as I preached.

With which of these two stories do you most readily identify? Are you like the lady who felt unqualified to open the Bible, thinking it is for the experts? Or are you a hungry Bible student who loves to hear good Bible teaching and is constantly taking notes? Perhaps you are somewhere in between! You are interested in the Bible but have no idea where to start reading or how to understand what you are reading. Maybe you pick up the Bible only during times of stress and open it at random hoping you will find an encouraging word. Wherever you are on this continuum, this book is written for you.

You will first be challenged to look at the benefits of studying God's Word. The Bible contains numerous promises that will encourage you to be faithful in your Bible study. We will also look at the attitudes that are necessary to be a student of the Word.

The first skill that must be learned is how to read the Bible for all it is worth. You will explore three different types of reading and learn how they relate to one another. You will discover eight questions you should ask of every text and eight questions you must ask yourself about every text. You will then focus on how to study an entire book and how to do a topical study. Various helpful appendices will help you to begin a relationship with God, tell you about the tools you should have to help you mine the gold in God's Word, provide links to reading plans to help you to organize your Bible study, and help you to master your new skills.

It is my desire and my prayer that this book will aid you in finding truth which is far more precious than gold. Let's start digging!

Ken Hemphill

The Benefits of and Attitudes for Bible Study

—✦—

The day before chapter 1 of this book was written, the largest lottery prize in history—1.6 billion dollars—was won. For the record I did not buy a ticket. The excitement generated by this jackpot had people standing in line for hours at a time at "lucky" sites to buy the tickets that would make someone, or a group of people, very wealthy. Just a guess, but I imagine you weren't the lucky winner who became an instant billionaire.

Here is a question to ponder: why would people line up overnight to buy a ticket that gave them infinitesimal odds of winning a jackpot? Now let's change the picture and the question. What if you discovered there was a vein of gold in your backyard? How much time and energy would you expend to mine that vein of gold? I suspect you would have a backhoe or two the next day. What if I told you that there is a vein of inexhaustible, pure gold available to you right now—gold that can be unearthed and produces true joy?

— READ PSALM 119. —

This book is about mining for gold, but the gold we will find is one that never perishes, which buys true happiness and blessings for this life and the one to come. The gold that is available to us is found in God's Word. Here's how the psalmist described the value of knowing and obeying God's Word: "Therefore I love Your commandments / Above gold, yes, above fine gold" (Ps. 119:127). Later he compares the understanding of God's Word with finding a great treasure: "I rejoice at Your word, / As one who finds great spoil" (v. 162). Think about it: our Creator has sent a love letter to us that details how we can live a purposeful life and enjoy His presence forever. Doesn't that make you want to dig for the gold contained inside?

In his search for wisdom the great and wealthy King Solomon received and passed on this sage counsel concerning God's Word:

> My son, if you will receive my words
> And treasure my commandments within you,
> Make your ear attentive to wisdom,
> Incline your heart to understanding . . .
> If you seek her as silver
> And search for her as for hidden treasure;
> Then you will discern the fear of the LORD
> And discover the knowledge of God." (Prov. 2:1–5)

God's Word contains treasures exceeding anything this world has to offer, but these treasures must be mined like gold and sought after like the great "treasures" they are. Effective Bible study requires diligent work, but it is joyous work that returns great riches. Do you agree with the psalmist when he wrote: "The law of Your mouth is better to me / Than thousands of gold and silver pieces"? (Ps. 119:72).

THE TOP 10 REASONS (PLUS 1) FOR STUDYING GOD'S WORD

1. *Studying the Bible allows us to know God intimately.* The Bible begins with the affirmation that man was created

by God in His own image (Gen. 1:27). The first chapters of Genesis make it clear that man was the zenith of God's creation. He placed man in a garden designed to provide for all his needs and gave him direct and intimate access to his Creator. Have you ever wondered what it means to be created in the image of God? Let me suggest a simple definition that may help you think about the awesome reality of being made in God's image. Human beings are *relational, rational,* and *responsible.* We are relational in that we are created to live in relationship with others and with our Creator. We are rational and therefore can understand the Creator when He communicates with us and this, in turn, makes human beings responsible to God. The Bible contains the story of God's revelation of Himself to humanity; it is the way He communicates with us. God's Word, along with prayer, are the primary means of communicating with God and therefore the way we get to know Him in an intimate, personal relationship.

The psalmist declared: "Establish Your word to Your servant, / As that which produces reverence for You" (Ps. 119:38). If you want to know God with growing intimacy, you must place a high priority on reading and studying His love letter to you.

2. *God's Word gives us guidance for daily living.* The Bible is described in many different ways. One of my favorites from childhood is found in Psalm 119:105, "Your word is a lamp to my feet / And a light to my path." My teachers explained that the "lamp" provides light on the path right before me to give me daily direction. The "light" for my path shines in front of me, providing direction for my life's journey. In other words, the lamp and light

will provide guidance for today and all my tomorrows. The psalmist picked up this theme of light again in verse 130: "The unfolding of Your words gives light; / It gives understanding to the simple."

Psalm 119 speaks of the psalmist's love for God's Word because "Your commandments make me wiser than my enemies . . . I have more insight than all my teachers, / For Your testimonies are my meditation. / I understand more than the aged, because I have observed Your precepts" (vv. 98–101). True wisdom is not found in academic degrees, one's IQ, or in age and experience; it is found in God's Word. The Bible will enable you to understand life and how to live it fully.

3. *God's Word equips us for meaningful service.* You were created with the wonderful privilege and potential for serving God, and the Bible will prepare you for effective service. Paul, writing to young Timothy declared: "All Scripture is inspired by God and profitable for teaching, for reproof, for correction, for training in righteousness; so that the man of God may be adequate, equipped for every good work" (2 Tim. 3:16–17). Did you notice the inclusive nature of the promise? The Word makes us "adequate . . . for *every* good work" (italics mine). Isn't that great news! You can be effective in doing that for which you were created—serving God through serving others.

Christians love to quote Ephesians 2:8–9, affirming our salvation by grace alone. Yet they often ignore the following verse that speaks of God's eternal purpose in our creation and redemption: "For we are His workmanship, created in Christ Jesus for good works, which God prepared beforehand so that we would walk in them"

(v. 10). The study of God's Word will enable you to know and accomplish that which God created you to be and saved you to accomplish.

4. *God's Word gives us assurance of salvation.* The fact that salvation is a free gift from a righteous God to the sinful human race may cause some to doubt whether something so wonderful can be true. A lack of assurance can create unnecessary fear and rob a person of the joy of living in an intimate relationship with God. John said that he wrote with a clear goal in mind: "These things I have written to you who believe in the name of the Son of God, so that you may know that you have eternal life" (1 John 5:13). You can *know,* not just *hope,* that you have eternal life. The psalmist declared the same truth: "Sustain me according to Your word, that I may live; / And do not let me be ashamed of my hope" (Ps. 119:116). Studying God's Word will yield the nugget of firm assurance that allows you to live a full and productive life.

As you study you will learn about God's character and know that His promises are fully trustworthy because they reflect His character. God cannot lie (Titus 1:2), and thus His promise to give eternal life to those who believe in Him becomes the bedrock foundation of one's life. Here is a promise that will calm your fears and anxiety: "My sheep hear My voice, and I know them, and they follow Me; and I give eternal life to them, and they will never perish; and no one will snatch them out of My hand" (John 10:27–28). We are doubly protected—because we have eternal life, we will not perish; and because God is all-powerful, no one can snatch us from His hand.

5. *Studying God's Word gives us confidence in prayer.* Bible study and prayer are companions when it comes to knowing God. Many Christians struggle in prayer because they lack the confidence that prayer actually matters. A few paragraphs earlier we looked at 1 John 5:13 concerning the assurance of salvation. This passage immediately connects the assurance of salvation to the confidence we can have in prayer. "This is the confidence which we have before Him, that, if we ask anything according to His will, He hears us. And if we know that He hears us in whatever we ask, we know that we have the requests which we have asked from Him" (vv. 14–15).

You may ask what is the relationship between confidence in prayer and Bible study. Jesus said, "If you abide in Me, and My words abide in you, ask whatever you wish, and it will be done for you" (John 15:7). God's Word abides in us as we study, meditate, and memorize it. We will encounter great men and women of prayer as we read God's Word. We can learn from the way they prayed and the results of their praying. We will find specific instruction on how to pray from the Master Himself. The study of the Bible makes us confident that God will answer our prayers according to His will as revealed in His Word.

6. *Studying God's Word brings cleansing from and victory over sin.* Nothing impedes intimacy with God like unconfessed sin (1 John 1: 6, 10), and nothing brings greater joy than the assurance that our sin has been forgiven. Listen to this promise: "But if we walk in the Light as He Himself is in the Light, we have fellowship with one another and the blood of Jesus His Son cleanses us from

all sin" (v. 7). John was affirming a fundamental truth: "If we confess our sins, He is faithful and righteous to forgive us our sins and to cleanse us from all unrighteousness" (v. 9).

Remember the author of 1 John also wrote the gospel of John. There he recorded the words of Jesus that show the connection between God's Word and the assurance of cleansing from sin. "You are already clean because of the word which I have spoken to you" (John 15:3). In His final prayer for His disciples of every generation, Jesus prayed, "Sanctify them in the truth; Your word is truth" (John 17:17).

The psalmist had much to say about the impact of God's Word as it relates to victory over sin:

> How can a young man keep his way pure?
> By keeping it according to Your word.
> With all my heart I have sought You;
> Do not let me wander from Your commandments.
> Your word I have treasured in my heart,
> That I may not sin against You. (Ps. 119:9–11)

One of the popular statements I heard often as a child was, "This book will keep you from sin, or sin will keep you from this book." The psalmist established this truth in a little more profound manner: "I have restrained my feet from every evil way, / That I may keep Your word. / Establish my footsteps in Your word, / And do not let any iniquity have dominion over me" (Ps. 119:101, 133). The attempt to live in victory over sin apart from regular Bible study is futile.

7. *Studying God's Word gives abiding joy and peace.* I find it curious and troubling that I encounter countless Christians who seem to lack both joy and peace. They allow

circumstances to dictate their lives and thus find themselves on a spiritual rollercoaster. They allow anxiety and fear to rob them of the joy of knowing and serving God.

Jesus' first-century disciples were thrown into inner turmoil by the news that it was necessary for Him to leave them. Jesus first comforted His disciples with the promise that someday they would be with Him forever. Despite this promise, they remained perplexed and anxious over their immediate status that they would be forced to live without His daily presence. He assured them that the Father would send another Helper who will be with them forever (John 14:16). The Holy Spirit would teach the disciples and bring to their remembrance all that Jesus taught them (v. 26). Notice the critical connection between the Word, the ministry of the Spirit, and the ongoing life of the disciples.

GOD'S PROMISES ARE FULLY TRUSTWORTHY BECAUSE THEY REFLECT HIS CHARACTER.

Immediately after the promise of the teaching ministry of the Spirit, Jesus declared, "Peace I leave with you; My peace I give to you; not as the world gives do I give to you. Do not let your heart be troubled, nor let it be fearful" (v. 27). In this same context Jesus declared; "These things I have spoken to you so that My joy may be in you, and that your joy may be made full" (15:11). As Jesus addressed the Father in the section we call the great High Priestly prayer, recorded in John 17, He reaffirmed the promise of joy and again connected it with God's Word. "But now I come to You; and these things I speak in the world so that they may have My joy made full in themselves. I have given them Your word"

(vv. 13–14a). *Our peace is assured and our joy is full because they come from God the Father and the Son, are mediated by the Holy Spirit, and are assured by His Word.*

The psalmist clearly understood the connection between God's Word and His abiding joy and perfect peace. He declared, "I have inherited Your testimonies forever, / For they are the joy of my heart. / Those who love Your law have great peace, / And nothing causes them to stumble" (Ps. 119:111, 165). If you desire joy and peace, you must love and study God's Word.

8. *Studying God's Word brings blessings.* Frequently I hear believers speak of their desire to have or experience God's blessing. Too often they speak of *blessing* in vague terms that makes blessing appear to be little more than a fuzzy, warm feeling they get during worship. Blessing is a bit more specific. When God established His covenant with Abraham, He promised to bless Abraham so that he could bless the nations. Further, God promised Abraham that He would be with him, protect him from his enemies, and provide for his needs. God's blessing is His *presence, provision,* and *protection.*

In Deuteronomy 11 we are told that blessing and cursing (the absence of blessing) involves a choice that is related specifically to hearing and obeying God's Word: "See, I am setting before you today a blessing and a curse: the blessing, if you listen to the commandments of the LORD your God, which I am commanding you today; and the curse, if you do not listen to the commandments of the LORD your God, but turn aside from the way which I am commanding you today, by following other gods which you have not known" (vv. 26–28). Blessing is obtained by hearing and obeying God's Word.

The psalmist clearly understood that God alone was "blessed" and was therefore the source of all blessing. For this reason, He asked God to teach him His statutes: "Blessed are You, O LORD; / Teach me Your statutes" (Ps. 119:12). God alone is the source of blessing, and He has chosen to mediate blessing through His Word.

It is impossible for us to think about blessing and not consult Jesus' Sermon on the Mount where He repeated the word *blessed* nine times. At the heart of the list is the promise that those who hunger and thirst for righteousness shall be satisfied. Blessing is the result of seeking God's righteousness, and our zeal for His righteousness will make us hunger and thirst for His Word.

9. *Studying God's Word enables us to explain our faith.* When we experience redemption, we have a genuine desire to tell others about our relationship to God and how they, too, can know Him. Yet studies indicate that a very small percentage of persons who claim to have a relationship with God have ever told anyone about it. The failure to share the good news is directly related to one's study of and confidence in God's Word. When we doubt the sufficiency of the Bible we are reluctant to share our faith.

Psalm 119:41–42 shows the dynamic relationship between salvation, sharing one's faith, and confidence in God's Word: "May Your lovingkindness also come to me, O LORD, / Your salvation according to Your word; / So I will have an answer for him who reproaches me, / For I trust in Your word." Peter established this same truth in his first letter. He spoke about the possibility of suffering for righteousness, which brings blessing (1 Peter 3:14). We are not to fear the world's intimidation nor are we to be troubled. What allows us to overcome our timidity? "But sanctify Christ as Lord in your hearts, always being ready to make a defense to everyone who asks you to give an account for the hope that is in you, yet with gentleness and reverence" (v. 15).

The effectiveness of our witness is not based on our cleverness, but on the power of God's Word. Paul called it "the power of God for salvation to everyone who believes" (Rom. 1:16). The more you know God's Word, the more confident and effective you will be in sharing the hope that is in you.

10. *Studying God's Word enables you to live successfully.* I can't imagine that anyone wants to be a failure in life. Of course we want to be successful. Many of the most popular and best-selling books promise to teach us how to be successful. Being successful doesn't necessarily mean fame and fortune; it means discovering God's purpose for your life and fulfilling it. The Bible teaches us how to be successful in life.

Joshua had been called upon to lead Israel into the promised land after the death of Moses. The Lord told Joshua that he must be strong and courageous if he was to succeed in this task:

> Only be strong and very courageous; be careful to do according to all the law which Moses My servant commanded you; do not turn from it to the right or to the left, so that you may have success wherever you go. This book of the law shall not depart from your mouth, but you shall meditate on it day and night, so that you may be careful to do according to all that is written in it; for then you will make your way prosperous, and then you will have success (Josh. 1:7–8).

The study of God's Word leads to obedience, and obedience leads to success.

In John 15:1–7 Jesus defined successful living in terms of the life that bears fruit. He affirmed that the branch cannot bear fruit by itself but only as it abides in the vine. He then declared, "I am the vine, you are the branches; he who abides in Me and I in him, he bears much fruit, for apart from Me you can do nothing" (John 15:5). This leads to an inevitable and critical question, how do I abide in Christ? Here is the answer in Jesus' own words, "If you abide in Me, and My words abide in you, ask whatever you wish, and it will be done for you" (v. 7). You cannot abide in God's Word unless you spend time in study, meditation, and memorization.

11. REVIVAL. This is the "plus" I promised. I think there is both a desperate need and heartfelt desire for revival in our day. The Christian community is in agreement that the health of our world, our nation, our communities, our churches, and our homes is dependent upon a revival. Truthfully, revival is first an individual matter before it can become a corporate one. Would you like to experience a true revival of your devotion and commitment to God? Would you like to be restored to your first love?

As I read through Psalm 119 in preparation to write this section, I began to notice that the word *revive* was repeated throughout the psalm:

> My soul cleaves to the dust;
> Revive me according to Your word.
> This is my comfort in my affliction,
> That Your word has revived me.
> Revive me according to Your lovingkindness,

So that I may keep the testimony of Your mouth.
I am exceedingly afflicted;
Revive me, O LORD according to Your word.
  (vv. 25, 50, 88, 107)

Toward the end of the psalm revival becomes a virtual refrain: "Hear my voice according to Your lovingkindness; / Revive me, O LORD, according to Your ordinances" (v. 149; cf. vv. 154, 156, 159). The key to genuine revival is the study of and obedience to God's Word. If you want personal revival, dig for the gold!

AS YOU BEGIN THIS JOURNEY OF MINING

FOR GOLD, STOP NOW AND ASK GOD

TO GIVE YOU A PERSONAL REVIVAL.

While these ten (plus one) reasons for studying God's Word should provide adequate motivation for a passionate study of the Bible, I would be remiss if I didn't mention that believers are commanded to study His Word. Paul wrote to young Timothy and exhorted him to be diligent in his study of God's Word "as a workman who does not need to be ashamed" (2 Tim. 2:15). Simply stated, the true believer will hunger for God's Word because we love God and desire to show it through our obedience. First Peter 2:2 indicates that those truly born of God's Spirit will hunger for the Word the way a newborn hungers for milk. By drinking the "pure milk of the word" we will "grow in respect to salvation."

THE SEVEN CRITICAL ATTITUDES FOR EFFECTIVE BIBLE STUDY

Before we deal with the *methods* for effective Bible study, we must address an issue that goes deeper and is more critical than method. That is one's attitude as he or she approaches God's Word. One who has the proper attitude will reap greater benefits from Bible study than the most brilliant scholar using good methodology. There have been noted scholars who have lectured on the Bible at the university and seminary levels, yet have not been transformed by the Author or the content of the Bible. These individuals approach the Bible as a "great book" without allowing the Holy Spirit to bring the truths within its pages to bear in their own lives. Whether we are preachers, teachers, or students, we can fall into the same trap if we are not careful.

Thus, from the beginning, we need to underline a critical truth about effective Bible study: *a person must be born again in order to enjoy effective and profitable Bible study.* It is true that an unsaved person may read and study the Bible and become quite knowledgeable about the historical facts contained inside. The unsaved person may profit by living by the principles taught in God's Word. But the Bible's purpose is to reveal God so that sinful humanity may live in intimate relationship with Him, and such understanding is made possible only through the ministry of the Holy Spirit.

THE BIBLE'S PURPOSE IS TO REVEAL GOD
SO THAT SINFUL HUMANITY MAY LIVE IN
INTIMATE RELATIONSHIP WITH HIM.

The Bible is a book that records God's words communicated to various authors by the Holy Spirit (more on this in the next chapter). For that reason it is fundamentally a spiritual book, and only a person who is born of the Spirit can fully comprehend its truth. The great apostle Paul explained clearly the process of the giving and understanding of God's Word in 1 Corinthians 2. He declared first that his preaching was not based on persuasive words containing worldly wisdom but was simply a demonstration of the Spirit and power so that the Corinthians' faith would be based on the power of God (vv. 1–5). Verse 9 speaks of the wonderful things that God has prepared for those who love Him, "things which eye has not seen and ear has not heard, / And which have not entered the heart of man." These cannot be ascertained through worldly wisdom:

> For to us God revealed them through the Spirit; for the Spirit searches all things, even the depths of God. For who among men knows the thoughts of a man except the spirit of the man which is in him? Even so the thoughts of God no one knows except the Spirit of God. Now we have received, not the spirit of the world, but the Spirit who is from God, so that we may know the things freely given to us by God, which things we also speak, not in words taught by human wisdom, but in those taught by the Spirit, combining spiritual thoughts with spiritual words" (vv. 10–13).

The last phrase of verse 13 can actually be translated "communicating spiritual truths to spiritual men."

Here is what you need to note:

1. The Bible is God's Word communicated by the Holy Spirit;

2. The Holy Spirit teaches spiritual truths to spiritual men;

3. When we are born again, we receive the Holy Spirit who will guide us into all truth.

The great commentator R. A. Torrey said it this way, "No mere knowledge of the human languages in which the Bible was written, however extensive and accurate it may be, will qualify one to understand and appreciate the Bible. One must understand the divine language in which it was written as well, the language of the Holy Spirit."[1] If you are not sure that you have been born again, read Appendix A. It will tell you how you can begin to have a personal relationship with God through Christ. If you have been born again, test your attitude against the following list.

1. *You must love God and His Word.* The goal of Bible study is to develop an intimate relationship with God; of greatest importance is that the student expresses love for God by loving His Word. The psalmist cried out, "Establish Your word to Your servant, / As that which produces reverence for You" (Ps. 119:38). Treat the Bible as a love letter from your Creator. This means that our default setting when studying God's Word is the assumption that it is an accurate and powerful message from God to us. Paul commended the Thessalonians for the manner in which they accepted the Word of God. "For this reason we also constantly thank God that when you received the word of God which you heard from us, you accepted it not as the word of men, but for what it really is, the word of God, which also performs its work in you who believe" (1 Thess. 2:13).

    Persons who love God's Word will approach their Bible study time as a delight rather than a duty or chore. Job spoke of his appetite for His Word: "I have treasured the words of His mouth more than my necessary food" (Job 23:12b). The psalmist frequently spoke of his love for the Word of God: "O how I love Your law! / It is my meditation all the day" (Ps. 119:97). When you receive a message from a loved one, you mull it over throughout the day; so it is with God's love letter to us. The writer

16

also compared it to food, declaring it to be sweeter than honey (v. 103). One reason for his love for God's Word is that he knows it to be "very pure" (v. 140). In other words it is God's truth without any mixture of human error. Psalm 119 concludes with, "Therefore I love Your commandments / Above gold, yes, above fine gold" (v. 127). If you love God you will love His Word.

2. *Your love will cause you to delight in His Word.* This attitude is closely related to the first one and flows from it. There is no question that I love my wife and kids, but there are times when I neglect them, and my relationship with them suffers because I failed to delight in them. The psalmist declared, "I shall delight in Your statutes; / I shall not forget Your word. / Your testimonies also are my delight; / They are my counselors" (119: 16, 24). The person who delights in the Word looks forward to his or her time of study and will find counsel within its pages. Too often we are quick to run to other sources for counsel before we seek it from the Bible.

PERSONS WHO LOVE GOD'S WORD WILL APPROACH THEIR BIBLE STUDY TIME AS A DELIGHT.

When we delight in the Word of God, we desire to respond with obedience. The writer of Psalm 119 said, "Make me walk in the path of Your commandments, / For I delight in it. / May Your compassion come to me that I may live, / For Your law is my delight" (vv. 35, 77). Delighting in God's Word allows us to understand His compassionate nature. We will desire to memorize it so we can meditate on it day and night. His Word becomes the joy of our hearts (v. 111).

3. *Approach your study time with a childlike mind.* As a pastor I loved to visit with the children of our church and talk with them about the Bible. They often had profound insights into God's Word because they accepted it as truth and took it at face value. They didn't approach the Word with preconceived notions or complicated theological systems that could cloud their understanding. They were not proud of their own understanding but were eager to learn. A child's faith is a simple one based on the reliability of God and His Word.

You may recall that in Jesus day, some of the best trained scholars—the scribes and Pharisees—failed to understand His teaching and embrace Him as the true Messiah. Matthew 11:25 tells us, "At that time Jesus said, 'I praise You, Father, Lord of heaven and earth, that You have hidden these things from the wise and intelligent and have revealed them to infants." God desires to reveal Himself to His children, so come to His Word as an expectant child.

Here is how the psalmist stated this truth: "The unfolding of Your words gives light; / It gives understanding to the simple" (Ps. 119:130). Just remember an infinite God knows infinitely more about life than you do! Approach God's Word with an open mind, and He will give you understanding.

AN INFINITE GOD KNOWS INFINITELY
MORE ABOUT LIFE THAN YOU DO!

4. *Saturate your study time with prayer.* A prayerful attitude demonstrates our total dependence and reminds us that we study His Word in His presence. R. A. Torrey

suggested that a person should read an entire book through while on his or her knees.[2] The issue is not one of posture but of attitude. It is a treat to get to know the author of any book and have him explain its meaning to you. Each time we open the Bible we have the privilege of studying His book in His presence and with His guidance. Prayer is like a flashlight that illumines the Word.

Here is a simple prayer you can pray to begin and end your Bible study time: "Open my eyes, that I may behold / Wonderful things from Your law" (Ps. 119:18). When you encounter those wonderful truths, take time to discuss them with your Father. Ask Him to help you remember His Word and apply it to your life. When we are conscious God made us and knows us intimately, it reminds us that only He can fully instruct us from His Word: "Your hands made me and fashioned me; / Give me understanding, that I may learn Your commandments" (v. 73).

5. *Be teachable.* This may sound obvious, but we need to be reminded that you can only teach those who are teachable. Jesus promised His disciples that after He departed, He would send the Holy Spirit to live within them. Jesus referred to the Holy Spirit as "the Spirit of truth" (John 14:17) because He would teach the disciples "all things" and bring His words to their memory (v. 26). As you pray, remember to ask God to teach you through His indwelling Spirit.

As you read Psalm 119 you will find that the psalmist's request that God teach him the Word was at the forefront of his mind:

Teach me Your statutes.
Make me understand the way of Your precepts,

So I will meditate on Your wonders.
Teach me, O LORD, the way of Your statutes,
And I shall observe it to the end.
Give me understanding, that I may observe Your law
And keep it with all my heart." (Ps. 119:26–27, 33–34)

Notice that he prays for understanding and the ability to obey. It is clear that the psalmist has found this to be a productive means of study: "I have not turned aside from Your ordinances, / For You Yourself have taught me" (vv. 102).

The psalmist's desire to allow God to teach him was based on his understanding that God manifests loving-kindness: "Deal with Your servant according to Your lovingkindness / And teach me Your statutes" (v. 124). He understood that God's Word gives life: "Your testimonies are righteous forever; / Give me understanding that I may live" (v. 144). Allowing God to be his teacher led the psalmist to give praise: "Let my lips utter praise, / For You teach me Your statutes" (v. 171). As you learn truth from God's Word, use that truth as a means of praising Him.

> PRAY THAT GOD
> WILL GIVE YOU A
> TEACHABLE SPIRIT!

6. *Respond with immediate and complete obedience.* While God's Word contains a wealth of *information,* its goal is *transformation.* James compared studying God's Word with looking in a mirror. This mirror not only reflects, but when the image contained therein is obeyed, it has the power to transform. He began by telling his readers to

put aside wickedness and receive the word with humility (James 1:21). Then he said,

> But prove yourselves doers of the word, and not merely hearers who delude themselves. For if anyone is a hearer of the word and not a doer, he is like a man who looks at his natural face in a mirror; for once he has looked at himself and gone away, he has immediately forgotten what kind of person he was. But one who looks intently at the perfect law, the law of liberty, and abides by it, not having become a forgetful hearer but an effectual doer, this man will be blessed in what he does. (vv. 22–25)

Approach Bible study with a humble spirit that desires to obey whatever truth God reveals.

The psalmist frequently expressed the attitude of humble obedience (Ps. 119:33–34). The desire to completely obey God's Word comes from a clear understanding of the very character of God who cannot and will not give bad gifts or do evil to His children (Luke 11:11–13). Our Creator desires that we experience abundant life, and His Word teaches us how to do so. The attitude of humble obedience leads to liberty and not bondage. Will you declare with the psalmist, "So I will keep Your law continually, / Forever and ever. / And I will walk at liberty, / For I seek Your precepts"? (119:44–45).

List any areas of disobedience that might prevent you from hearing and responding to God's Word. Ask God to cleanse you.

_____

_____

Here is a verse that you can use as a covenant to end your Bible study time each day: "I have sworn and I will confirm it, / That I will keep Your righteous ordinances" (Ps. 119:106). God's ordinances are righteous because they reflect His character; thus obedience to them is the only sensible response of the child of God. Remember: delayed obedience is present disobedience and partial obedience is total disobedience.

7. *Be willing to dig for the gold.* Bible study is a privilege and a delight, but it is also hard work. Are you willing to do the work necessary to know God and experience His blessing? The great prophet Jeremiah spoke of consuming God's Word: "Your words were found and I ate them, / And Your words became for me a joy and the delight of my heart; / For I have been called by Your name, / O LORD God of hosts" (Jer. 15:16).

The book of Psalms begins with a description of the "blessed" man:

> How blessed is the man who does not walk in the
>   counsel of the wicked,
> Nor stand in the path of sinners,
> Nor sit in the seat of scoffers!
> But his delight is in the law of the LORD,
> And in His law he meditates day and night." (1:1–2)

It takes time and effort to study and meditate on God's Word, but the result is clearly worth the work. Psalm 1:3 says, "He will be like a tree firmly planted by streams of water, / Which yields its fruit in its season / And its leaf does not wither; / And in whatever he does, he prospers."

Read all of Proverbs 2 where Solomon explains both the work necessary to know God's commandments and the blessing derived from the work. Verses 4–5 say, "If you seek her as silver / And search for her as hidden treasures; / Then you will discern the fear of the Lord / And discover the knowledge of God."

WHAT A PROMISE!

MINE THE GOLD

1. Read Proverbs 2 and note the connections between God's commandments and His blessings.

2. Memorize 1 Peter 2:2.

3. Sign and date this covenant:

"I have sworn and I will confirm it, that I will keep Your righteous ordinances."

Signed _____

Date _____

Getting to Know Your Bible

Our first step in learning to mine for gold is to become thoroughly acquainted with our Bibles. The Bible, the written record of God's revelation of Himself to humanity, is crucial to our understanding of God and the world He created. The Bible doesn't simply add to our theological knowledge; it is central to all knowledge and provides the grid by which we evaluate all other knowledge. We may learn about God from observing nature, and through our own conscience, but the Bible is the only complete source for knowing about God and His plan for our lives. For that reason, we can speak of Christ as the living Word of God (John 1:1) and the Bible as the written Word of God.

Throughout the history of the church, leaders have spoken of Scripture as the final and sufficient rule of faith and practice. This means that Scripture becomes the point of reference and final authority by which all beliefs, and their accompanying patterns of behavior, must be evaluated. Therefore it is critical that we first cover essential truths about the Bible, how to choose a Bible, and how to familiarize yourself with the Bible you will be studying.

SIX ESSENTIAL TRUTHS ABOUT THE BIBLE

1. *The Bible is God's revelation to humanity.* The first question we need to ask ourselves is how a limitless God could communicate with limited humans. The word *revelation* simply means that the content of Scripture was given to humans by God. The Bible is not a story about humanity trying to find or explain God; it is the story of God explaining Himself to humanity. In Romans 1:19–20, Paul indicated that God reveals Himself in nature and through the human conscience. This is referred to as *general revelation.* General revelation is sufficient to condemn humans but not sufficient to save us. The human race requires more direct and specific revelation to understand the character and will of God. The Bible is God's spoken word to humans, which He spoke through human instruments in both the Old and New Testaments to tell the story of His redemptive activity in human history.

The writer of Hebrews stated that God spoke first through the prophets, and finally and fully, He spoke in the person of His Son. "God, after He spoke long ago to the fathers in the prophets, in many portions and many ways, in these last days has spoken to us in His Son, whom He appointed heir of all things, through whom also He made the world. And He is the radiance of His glory and the exact representation of His nature, and upholds all things by the word of His power" (1:1–3a). Since Jesus is fully God, nothing can be added to the full revelation contained in the Bible we have in our hands. Some popular movies and cults are based on "lost" or "forgotten" books of the Bible. Don't be taken in. God's complete and final word was spoken in His Son. There are no hidden books that would add to the revelation made complete and final in Christ and contained in the Bible. Ask yourself, "How could God lose something He wrote and protected?"

When we use the word *revelation* we are saying that the *content* of Scripture originated with God and not humans. Here's how Peter explained it: "But know this first of all, that no prophecy of Scripture is a matter of one's own interpretation, for no prophecy was ever made by an act of human will, but men moved by the Holy Spirit spoke from God" (2 Peter 1:20–21). None of the human authors took it upon themselves to explain God nor did they attempt to explain Him with their own ideas. Exodus 17:14 tells us how Moses wrote the first five books of the Bible: "Then the LORD said to Moses, 'Write this in a book as a memorial and recite it to Joshua.'" The words, once given, were not to be added to or taken from in any way (Deut. 4:2). David was the author of significant portions of the Old Testament. He indicated clearly that the words he spoke and recorded were given to Him by God: "The Spirit of the LORD spoke by me, / And his word was on my tongue" (2 Sam. 23:2). Peter indicated that the Holy Spirit put words in the mouth of David that foretold the betrayal by Judas (Acts 1:16). The prophet Jeremiah spoke of his preaching and writing in graphic language: "Then the LORD stretched out His hand and touched my mouth, and the LORD said to me, 'Behold, I have put My words in your mouth'" (Jer. 1:9).

Clearly the authors of the New Testament treated the Old Testament as being the authoritative Word of God. Jesus considered the Old Testament as authoritative

(Matt. 21:42) and declared that the Old Testament pointed to Him (Luke 24:27). In the Sermon on the Mount, Jesus affirmed the enduring nature of the law down to the smallest detail. He submitted Himself to Scripture and yet taught with the authority of Scripture (Matt. 7:29). The disciples treated the words of the Lord as having the same authority as Old Testament Scriptures (Acts 20:35). On two different occasions New Testament authors cited other New Testament books as having scriptural authority (1 Tim. 5:18; 2 Peter 3:16). Paul's declaration in 1 Corinthians 14:37 indicates he was aware that his writings had scriptural authority: "If anyone thinks he is a prophet or spiritual, let him recognize that the things which I write to you are the Lord's commandment."

You may hear someone speak of *progressive* revelation. This simply means that God's revelation to humans became more complete and clear with the progression of time. The writer of Hebrews told of God speaking "in many portions and in many ways" through the prophets (1:1). He then contrasted Old Testament revelation with the final and complete revelation through God's Son. Progressive revelation does not suggest that God withheld revelation but that He revealed as much as human beings could process at any given time. The limitation was not with the desire or ability of God but in the ability of humans to fully comprehend. To illustrate this, you might think of the way you reveal your desires to preschoolers, preteens, or high school students. As they mature and respond to you as a parent, you give them greater opportunity and responsibility.

One reason that Bible study is so essential to spiritual growth is that the Bible contains the very words of God as He speaks to every area of life. This is God's love letter to His children.

2. *The Bible is inspired by God.* The word *inspiration* refers to the transmission of the content of Scripture from God to humans through those who spoke and recorded God's message. The use of inspiration in regard to Scripture does not mean the authors of Scripture had a burst of insight as a songwriter or poet; but it affirms that God, who provided the content, selected, protected, and enabled writers to record His message. Paul declared: "All Scripture is inspired by God" (2 Tim. 3:16). Some English translations read "God-breathed," indicating that both the source of Scripture and the means of transmission were accomplished by God.

The twin truths of revelation and inspiration are affirmed in 2 Peter 1:21, "For no prophecy was ever made by an act of human will, but men moved by the Holy Spirit spoke from God." The phrase "spoke from God" refers to *revelation,* indicating the content originated with God, and the phrase "moved by the Holy Spirit" points to *inspiration.* In other words, God prompted men to speak and write, gave them the words, and moved them along in the process of speaking and recording His words. The Holy Spirit took the initiative, and the men cooperated with the Spirit.

The Bible is distinct from other "holy books" because it was not an act of human initiative. It does not contain a human attempt to discover or explain God. In the process of revelation, God did not destroy the personality of the human instruments but rather guided, controlled, and protected the authors from error. Since God chose to use human authors, they spoke and wrote in the normal language and idioms of their day. They sometimes paraphrased in quotations, rounded off numbers, and employed language readily understood by their audience. They used figures of speech and illustrations common to their times and geographical locations. As you read the prophetic books, the Gospels, or the Epistles, you will find that writing styles vary greatly. This was necessary because God desired to speak to humans in a manner we could fully and easily understand. On occasions the authors were prompted by the Spirit to use sources. Luke tells us that he carefully investigated what others had written before he wrote his account (Luke 1:1–4). This process of *dynamic inspiration*, which indicates that God used human instruments to convey His truth, makes Bible study necessary and exciting.

THE BIBLE WRITERS:

- Used normal language and idiomatic expressions
- Sometimes paraphrased in quotations
- Rounded off numbers
- Employed language readily understood by their audience
- Used figures of speech and recognizable illustrations
- Had individual styles of writing that varied greatly
- Sometimes used sources

While inspiration is used primarily to explain how the Bible was given to humankind and kept free from error, it can also be used to indicate that God can inform our minds as we read and study His Word today. As we saw in the first chapter, the same Holy Spirit who inspired the original authors will be your guide as you dig for gold.

3. *The Bible is trustworthy.* When speaking of the Bible as both accurate and trustworthy, we can use the words *infallible* and *inerrant.* In classical usage *infallibility* speaks of the trustworthiness of a guide who is not deceived and does not deceive. Think of it in these terms: If you were taking a hike in a wilderness area unfamiliar to you, you would want to hire a guide who was fully trustworthy. If not, he could easily take advantage of you in the wilderness. Since your survival depends on this guide, you want to make sure that he is not easily confused, nor would he deceive you. You want an infallible guide. Nothing in the Bible will ever mislead you, so you can obey it with joyous abandon.

The word *inerrant* speaks of the truthfulness of a source of information. Simply stated, does it contain mistakes? When we affirm that the Bible is inerrant, we are affirming that when we understand it properly in the context of its ancient cultural form and content, it is completely truthful in all it says about God's will and way. If the Bible contained errors, humanity would need an inerrant interpreter to detect which passages are flawed and which are reliable. God so loved the world that He provided a book that is completely reliable.

GOD SO LOVED THE WORLD THAT
HE PROVIDED A BOOK THAT IS
COMPLETELY RELIABLE.

Let's think about our wilderness trip again. We have established that our guide is trustworthy and therefore would not intentionally deceive us. But what if the map our guide was using contained mistakes? Even though he fully intended to guide us safely, he would lead us astray based on a faulty map. We want a guide whose information is inerrant. The knowledge that our map— the Bible—is without error gives us confidence in life and death.

The psalmist referred to the Scripture as "the word of truth" (119:43) and declares, "Forever, O LORD, / Your word is settled in heaven" (v. 89). Jesus indicated that it would be easier for heaven and earth to pass away than for the smallest detail of the law to fail (Luke 16:17). In Revelation John declared that God affirmed "these words are faithful and true" (22:6), and then he concluded by warning about adding to or taking from the words in his book (22:18–19).

Those who challenge inerrancy often do so because of their anti-supernatural bias. They dismiss any miracle and thus cannot accept that God could communicate his truth through a human instrument without it containing error. Further they demand a rigid understanding of the text that they would not apply to other documents. I once knew a liberal professor who made fun of people who believed the Bible was literally true. He then stated that Jesus indicated that He was the "door" (John 10:7, 9). He wanted to know if he was a wood door, a screen door, and so forth. He also spoke of the glaring scientific error contained in the assertion in Scripture about the sun rising (Ps. 19:6). Apparently he didn't watch television since weather forecasters make this same assertion daily. Figures of speech and other normal uses of language do not constitute error.

THE TWO CRITICAL QUESTIONS

Would God desire to reveal Himself accurately?

Could God reveal Himself accurately?

When dealing with the subject of the trustworthiness of Scripture, I ask two questions. First, if God desired to reveal Himself to humans, would he do so in a totally accurate (inerrant) and reliable (infallible) way? The word *would* indicates "intent" or "desire." The only possible answer is yes, for the God revealed in Scripture is neither deceitful nor capricious. He is not a "trickster" like the Roman and Greek gods. The God of the Bible is righteous and thus *would* reveal Himself in a manner consistent with His own nature. If such is not true, humanity is hopeless, for we are unqualified to match wits with a god who desires to deceive us.

IF GOD DID NOT DESIRE TO REVEAL HIMSELF
ACCURATELY, HUMANITY IS HOPELESS SINCE
WE ARE UNQUALIFIED TO MATCH WITS WITH
A GOD WHO DESIRES TO DECEIVE US!

After resolving the previous question, we ask: *Could* God reveal Himself in an accurate way and fully protect that revelation? The word *could* speaks to "ability." Some liberal thinkers argue that we cannot have an inerrant text because of the fallible human instruments God used. Such a suggestion leaves us in an untenable situation. We would then have a God who *desires* to reveal Himself to His own creation in a reliable and accurate manner but is *incapable* of doing so. In other words, God is *finite* or limited in His ability. Yet, as we read the Bible, it is clear that the God of the Bible is not limited.

The God who created the world, entered that world in human flesh through His Son, and raised Jesus from the grave is also able to protect His written revelation from error. To suggest that He *could* not do so is both a weak and illogical position, since the writers of Scripture would have invented a God (in their own minds) greater than the One they affirmed commissioned them to write. To argue that He *would* not do so would make him cruel and petty. When we conclude that God *would* and *could* protect His word, we are left with the historical position of evangelical Christianity—the Bible is inerrant and infallible.

When inerrancy is rejected, we are less sure of the value of Scripture, less certain of our own faith, and more susceptible to alternative truth claims. When we affirm the authority, truthfulness, and sufficiency of Scripture it should motivate us to study it with passion, to commit ourselves to the process of mining the gold.

4. *The Bible is powerful.* While the issues of revelation, inspiration, and trustworthiness are important to all

believers, the understanding that the Bible is powerful should provide the motivation to study it and the confidence to obey it. We can read a great classic or a moving poem and be inspired or moved to tears, but no other book has the power to transform us.

Here are a few statements about the power inherent in God's Word that are worth committing to memory:

The Word will accomplish God's purposes. "For as the rain and the snow come down from heaven, / And do not return there without watering the earth / And making it bear and sprout, / And furnishing seed to the sower and bread to the eater; / So will My word be which goes forth from My mouth; / It will not return to Me empty, / without accomplishing what I desire, / And without succeeding in the matter for which I sent it" (Isa. 55:10–11).

The Word is the power of God for salvation. "For I am not ashamed of the gospel, for it is the power of God for salvation to everyone who believes, to the Jew first and also to the Greek" (Rom. 1:16).

The Word equips us for ministry. "All Scripture is inspired by God and profitable for teaching, for reproof, for correction, for training in righteousness; so that the man of God may be adequate, equipped for every good work" (2 Tim. 3:16–17).

The Word judges our thoughts and attitudes. "For the word of God is living and active and sharper than any two-edged sword, and piercing as far as the division of soul and spirit, of both joints and marrow, and able to judge the thoughts and intentions of the heart" (Heb. 4:12).

All of these verses indicate that the Word has the power to accomplish the stated result. The study of God's Word is critical to our spiritual development because it has the power to change our lives.

5. *The Bible is totally sufficient.* The Bible is God's guide-book for living successfully. We have already seen this in several of the verses from Psalm 119, but it is worth repeating. Living successfully means that we accomplish the purpose for which we were created. We were created in God's image so that we might have intimate fellowship with Him now and for all eternity. We are gifted and empowered to join Him in His kingdom activity. The Bible is not simply a book of history; it is a book of life. Through it God provides us with clear guidelines and laws which govern every activity of life. The Bible addresses sexual purity, marriage, parenting, money management, business ethics, and every other topic of relevance to living an abundant life. Thus our study will not simply reveal important biblical facts; it will provide instruction concerning everything we need to know about life.

THE BIBLE IS NOT SIMPLY A BOOK OF
HISTORY; IT IS A BOOK OF LIFE.

6. *The Bible has been preserved in a reliable form.* I am asked occasionally whether the Bible in my hand is trustworthy. This question speaks to the topic of the preservation of the text. We do not have any original autograph or first copy. For example, we do not have the original handwritten copy of Romans from the pen of

Paul. The same is true for any first-century or earlier document. What the reader wants to know is whether we can have confidence that the Bible we are studying contains an accurate record of what the Holy Spirit spoke through Paul.

While no original autographs have survived, we do have a large number of quality early manuscripts. In the case of the Old Testament, the Hebrew texts are unusually well-preserved. They have proved themselves to be exceptionally reliable—a fact supported by the Dead Sea Scrolls.

With more than five thousand Greek and eight thousand Latin manuscripts, no other book in ancient literature can compare with the New Testament in terms of documentary support. For example, we have only seven early copies of Plato's writings, five of Aristotle's, and 643 of Homer's. It is interesting that some college professors, who cast doubt on the reliability of the Bible by citing the issue of manuscripts, accept without question the reliability of the words of Plato or Aristotle in spite of the few manuscripts that exist.

The quality of the various Old and New Testament manuscripts is without parallel in the ancient world. The reverence that the Jewish scribes and early Christian copyists had for Scripture caused them to exercise extreme care as they copied and preserved the original texts. Because we do have thousands of manuscripts, readings may vary in places. The differences are often little more than the spelling of names or other small variances, the result of visual or auditory errors in the copying process. Many modern translations will indicate in a footnote when there is a manuscript difference and tell you what other reading exists. Only a minute number would affect one's understanding of the text, and none call into question a major doctrine or factual teaching.

Another related question concerns whether our listing of sixty-six books is complete. This question has been raised by popular movies and documentaries on The History Channel and others that supplement the story of the Bible with books that were written between the Old and New Testaments and after the time of the close of the New Testament. These books are called the Apocrypha and pseudepigrapha. *Apocrypha* means "things which are hidden." The Apocryphal books were written by Jews in the time between the Testaments. They do contain important information about this time period but were never considered to be canonical by the Jewish community that produced them. They are accepted by the Roman Catholic Church but have been omitted by Protestant churches since the time of the Reformation. *Pseudepigrapha* means "false writings," and many were attributed to ancient heroes such as Adam, Enoch, or Moses. While these writings may have value in helping one understand the background of the New Testament, they are not viewed as having canonical authority.

You may have heard of the canon of Scripture. The word *canon* means "rule" or "standard" and came to mean the collection of authentic Scriptures. The actual composition of the New Testament writings began in the late AD 40s and proceeded throughout the latter half of the first century. The process of canonization is best understood as the "recognition" by the church of the

Scriptures that God chose to inspire. Most of the books of the New Testament were recognized and used regularly by the early first century. The second century was pivotal in the process of canonization, and by the end of that century the twenty-seven books of the New Testament were largely agreed upon. Several criteria were employed by the early church fathers to determine which books should be included.

First was the direct or indirect association of a written work with an apostle. This list would include Matthew, John, Peter (Matt. 10:2–3), Paul, and James and Jude, the half brothers of Jesus. We would include Mark indirectly as a close associate of Peter and Luke as a traveling companion of Paul. Second was the question as to whether the teaching conformed to the church's rule of faith. A third matter was antiquity. Was the writing produced during the lifetime of the original eyewitnesses? This would exclude all second- and third-century apocryphal and pseudepigraphal literature such as the Gospel of Thomas or the Shepherd of Hermas. A final issue was how widely the materials were used by the early church.

CRITERIA FOR CANONIZATION

1. Association with an apostle
2. Teaching conformed with the church's rule of faith
3. Was it produced in the lifetime of the original eyewitnesses?
4. Widespread use by the early church

You can be confident that the Bible you hold in your hands today contains all that God intended to be contained in Holy Scriptures. Further, you can know that it accurately reflects that which He communicated to the original authors.

THE BIBLE YOU HOLD IN YOUR HANDS TODAY CONTAINS ALL THAT GOD INTENDED TO BE CONTAINED IN THE HOLY SCRIPTURES.

SELECTING AND GETTING ACQUAINTED WITH YOUR BIBLE

Choosing a Bible

The first essential task in preparing to discover gold is the selection of a study Bible. This will be our primary tool since we must always begin with Bible reading. Anyone who does not read the Hebrew and Greek texts will study the Bible from a *translation*. Fortunately, there are many wonderful translations available to the Bible student today.

Essentially there are three different options for you to choose from. The *word-for-word* translation is a "literal translation" or a "formal equivalence." Examples of a formal equivalence would be the King James Version (KJV), the New King James Version (NKJV), the New American Standard Bible (NASB), the Holman Christian Standard Bible (HCSB), the New Revised Standard Version (NRSV), and the English Standard Version (ESV). Word-for-word translations attempt to preserve the original syntax and exact meaning of the words without sacrificing readability. The advantage of the word-for-word translation is that it preserves the original wording and gives you a flavor of the individual author's style. The possible disadvantage is that a word-for-word translation can in fact be difficult to read. As you progress in your Bible study skills, you will want to own several different Bibles, and you should have one from this category. You might want to ask your pastor which translation he uses for preaching or ask your teacher which translation is being used in your small group.

THE FIRST ESSENTIAL TASK IN PREPARING TO DISCOVER GOLD IS THE SELECTION OF A STUDY BIBLE.

At the other end of the spectrum is the paraphrase. The original Living Bible by Kenneth Taylor (TLB), Good News Translation (GNT), and The Message by Eugene Peterson (MSG) are examples of popular paraphrases. The paraphrase takes great liberty with the text, and is generally used for devotional reading, but does not make a good study Bible. The strength of the paraphrase is that it is easy to use and understand. The weakness is that it does not always accurately represent the exact meaning of the text.

The *dynamic equivalence* translations lie between the two. The translators attempt to make the Bible more understandable by translating thought-for-thought without moving into paraphrasing. The New International Version (NIV), the New English Translation (NET), J. B. Phillips New Testament in Modern English (PHILLIPS), the New Living Translation (NLT), and The Voice Bible (VOICE) are good examples. The strength of the dynamic equivalence is their readability and their ability of making idiomatic expressions clear. You will profit from having one of these translations to use alongside your word-for-word translation.

THREE TYPES OF TRANSLATIONS

WORD-FOR-WORD TRANSLATION	PARAPHRASE	DYNAMIC EQUIVALENCE
KJV	TLB	NIV
NKJV	GNT	NET
NASB	MSG	PHILLIPS
HCSB		NLT
NRSV		VOICE
ESV		

Becoming familiar with your Bible

Start by opening your Bible to the table of contents. You will notice that the Bible has two major divisions: the Old Testament and the New Testament. The Old Testament contains thirty-nine books, and the New Testament has twenty-seven. The Old Testament contains the promise of the Messiah, and the New Testament contains the fulfillment of that promise. Both contain salvation history, and both are fully inspired and totally reliable.

I find it helpful to make notes in my Bible. I would suggest that you mark your table of contents with the major divisions of the Bible, which we will discover below. If you prefer not to write in your Bible, you might want to copy the page and make a similar chart to insert in your Bible at this point.

When we use the term *Old* Testament it doesn't mean outdated, less inspired, or less profitable. It simply refers to the first "testament" or "covenant" God made with Israel. The study of the Old Testament is essential to our full understanding of God's story of redemption.

The first five books of the Old Testament are referred to as the Pentateuch (a five-scrolled book) or Torah (law or teaching). These books cover salvation history from the very beginning of time through the entry into the promised land. The books are foundational and fundamental, including the story of the patriarchs, the redemption and making of a nation, and the giving of the law. Moses is considered to be the primary author of this material.

The Pentateuch is followed by twelve historical books, beginning with Joshua and ending with Esther. These books follow the story of God's people beginning with the entry into the promised land. They recount the time of the judges and the kings (including the united and divided kingdoms), the Babylonian captivity, and the return from exile.

In the middle of the Old Testament are five books of poetry and wisdom literature. Included are Job, Psalms, Proverbs, Ecclesiastes, and the Song of Solomon, sometimes called Song of Songs.

The final two sections are referred to as the Major Prophets which includes Isaiah, Jeremiah, Lamentations, Ezekiel, and Daniel. The Minor Prophets follow, beginning with Hosea and concluding with Malachi. The chief difference between the major and minor prophets is the length of their books and not the relative value. All the prophets were spokesmen for God. Much of the content of their messages was clearly intended for the people and time in which they lived. However, some of their messages contained prophecy which found its ultimate fulfillment in future events, including the promise of a coming Messiah.

The New Testament begins with the four gospels and the book of Acts, which provide the historical framework of the life of Christ and His continuing work through the church. Matthew, Mark, and Luke are referred to as the Synoptic Gospels, because they view Jesus' life from a chronological perspective. John's material is organized around "sign" events in the life of Jesus. Luke and Acts is actually a two-volume work by a single author: Luke's gospel tells the life of Christ from beginning through the resurrection, and Acts tells of the birth and empowering of the church as the continuing ministry of the risen Christ.

The apostle Paul wrote thirteen of our New Testament letters, sometimes referred to as the Pauline Epistles. Most were letters addressed to the early churches he planted as the first great missionary. The letters to Timothy, Titus, and Philemon are more personal in nature. The General Epistles include Hebrews, James, First and Second Peter, First, Second, and Third John, and Jude. The final book, Revelation, is prophetic in nature and tells of the culmination of all things.

DIVISIONS OF THE OLD AND NEW TESTAMENTS

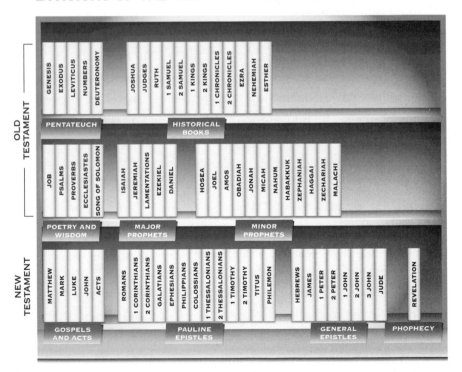

Getting the Big Picture

Having an overall view of the story line of the Bible is helpful. There are several ways to go about this, but I am going to use the one provided by Vaughn Roberts in his book *God's Big Picture.*[1] Vaughn bases his overview on the theme of the kingdom of God, which is the dominant theme of Jesus' teaching ministry. Jesus cast His mission in terms of fulfilling the promises of the coming King and His kingdom. Although the term "kingdom of God" does not appear in the Old Testament, the idea certainly does. Here is a brief synopsis of the big picture of God's kingdom activity. For a more complete understanding of the story line of the Bible, I recommend that you add this book to your gold mining tool kit.

🪨 THE OLD TESTAMENT

A. **The pattern of the kingdom.** The garden of Eden established the pattern of the kingdom. Adam and Eve were allowed to live in God's place under His rule. To be under God's rule is to enjoy His blessing. This is God's design for humanity and thus the best way to live abundantly.

B. **The perished kingdom.** Tragically, Adam and Eve believed they could live more abundantly by ignoring God's rule. The results were tragic as they hid from God. They forfeited God's place as they were banished from the garden, and they forfeited God's blessings when they removed themselves from God's rule. While the situation seemed desperate, God was determined to restore His kingdom.

C. **The promised kingdom.** God made a covenant with Abraham and his descendants that included His plan to reestablish His kingdom. They were to live in His land

and enjoy His blessing so that all the people of the earth would be blessed through them.

D. The partial kingdom. God's promises to Abraham were only partially fulfilled in Israel. By redeeming the Israelites from Egyptian bondage, God made Abraham's descendants His own people. At Mount Sinai, He gave them His law so they could live under His rule and enjoy His blessing. This blessing was marked by God's presence as symbolized by the tabernacle. Under Joshua's leadership, the people entered the promised land and enjoyed peace and prosperity during the reigns of kings David and Solomon. This was the high point for Israel—they were God's people, in God's place, under God's rule, enjoying God's blessing. However, the promise to Abraham had not been fulfilled completely because the Israelites disobeyed God's law continually and neglected the commission to bless the nations. Their stubborn disobedience led to the demise of the partial kingdom as Israel was divided.

E. The prophesied kingdom. After the death of Solomon, civil war broke out, and the kingdom was divided—Israel in the north and Judah in the south. After two hundred years of separate existence, the Northern Kingdom was destroyed by the Assyrians. The Southern Kingdom limped on for another century; then it, too, was captured, and the people were taken exile to Babylon. During this depressing period, God spoke to the people of Israel and Judah through prophets, explaining that they were being punished for sin. However God offered hope for a future kingdom. The prophets pointed expectantly to a time when God would send His anointed King (Messiah) who would fulfill all His promises and establish His kingdom. The Old Testament ends with the people waiting for God's King to appear.

THE NEW TESTAMENT

F. The present kingdom. Four hundred years of silence by God followed the promises of Malachi, the last of the Old Testament prophets. John the Baptist heralded the coming of the kingdom with a call for repentance. Jesus began His public ministry with the words, "The time has come . . . the kingdom of God has come near" (Mark 1:15 NIV). Jesus' life and teaching proved He was the promised King. Yet the King chose a surprising way of establishing God's kingdom—His own death on the cross. By His death, Jesus dealt with the problem of sin and made it possible for humans to live in relationship with the holy God. Jesus' resurrection from the dead demonstrated the success of His mission and proclaimed hope for all the nations.

G. The proclaimed kingdom. The death and resurrection of the King accomplished everything necessary to completely restore God's kingdom. However, He did not usher in His completed kingdom during His earthly ministry. He ascended into heaven, indicating there would be a delay before His triumphant return to establish His perfected kingdom. The delay provides time for all the peoples of the earth to hear the good news so they can live under His rule and reign. The period of the "last days" began with Pentecost when God sent His Spirit to empower and equip His church to take the message to the ends of the earth. We are still living in this age and are to participate in the proclamation of His kingdom.

H. The perfected kingdom. One day Christ will return as the triumphant King. There will be a final division when His enemies will be separated from His presence and rule as they are cast into hell. But all born-again believers will join him in a perfect new creation. Revelation, the final book of the Bible, describes a fully restored kingdom where God's people from every nation will be in God's place, under His rule, enjoying His blessing forever.

Doesn't God's plan for His kingdom excite you? Learning how to study the Bible for yourself will assist you in understanding God's big plan and how you fit into that plan. God has a purpose for your life, and He wants to reveal it to you as you study His Word.

MINE THE GOLD

1. If you don't already know the books of the Bible, begin to memorize them in order.

2. If you are comfortable writing in your Bible, mark the table of contents, denoting the various divisions in the Old and New Testaments.

3. See what Bibles you already own, and consider buying an additional Bible to add to your toolbox.

4. Go online and download an audio Bible in the translation of your choice. If you need suggestions, refer to the translations mentioned in this chapter.

Reading the Bible for All Its Worth

Before you can study God's Word you have to make a firm commitment to read it. Reading is the fundamental implement in our tool bag as we dig for gold. Before you complain that you don't like to read, or that you are not a good reader, let me remind you we are referring to a love letter from God to us that promises to provide everything necessary for us to live successfully. If you don't like to read, ask the Holy Spirit to give you the desire and to change your attitude. The very process of reading will improve your ability to read and thus cause you to enjoy it more.

I heard a story once about a young, single lady who decided to take a cruise alone. She had taken a popular new novel with her to read on her deck chair. She struggled through the first and second chapters, and she simply couldn't get anything out of the book. One evening at dinner she was seated with an attractive man about her own age, and sparks began to fly. As they were getting better acquainted during the ensuing days, she asked her new friend what he did for a living. To her surprise and delight, she found that he was an author. In fact, he was the author who had written the novel she had put aside a few days earlier. When the evening ended, she hastily retreated to her

cabin and began to devour the novel. To her absolute surprise and delight she found the novel fascinating. In fact, she
couldn't put it down. What had happened? She had met the
author and was falling in love with him. If you know and
love the Author of the Bible, you will have a passion to read
God's love letter.

THREE MAJOR TYPES OF READING

There is more than one way to read the Bible, and thus it is
helpful to distinguish between these ways of reading before
we talk about developing consistency in our Bible reading.

1. *Devotional reading.* Devotional reading is usually brief
   by design and may employ devotional guides and devotional patterns. The guides may vary greatly, but most
   usually have a central verse with a short devotional
   thought to help you understand and apply the verse.
   Devotional reading may also follow a scriptural pattern
   such as reading a proverb or psalm each day. Some persons use a diary or notebook as they do their devotional
   reading so they can record their response or praise to
   God. Devotional reading is important and should not be
   ignored, but it is somewhat like an energy snack that we
   eat between meals—it should never stand alone since
   it does not provide a balanced diet. Devotional reading may actually provide you with ideas that will lead to
   survey or study reading.

2. *Survey reading.* Survey reading consists of planned
   reading through chapters, books, or the entire Bible over
   a certain period of time. There are many different plans
   that allow you to read through the Bible in a certain
   period of time, and such a project should be undertaken
   by every serious Bible student on a regular basis (see

Appendix C for suggested reading plans). Other forms of survey reading may prompt you to read a certain book over a set period of time, which will require that you read a few chapters per day. Popular books for this type of reading are Psalms, Paul's letters, and the Gospels, but I would hasten to say that every book of the Bible contains truth valuable for the growing Christian. Thus you should not hesitate to tackle any and every book of the Bible. Once again, I would recommend that you have a simple notebook handy to record what you have read and what God said to you. Writing a truth down will help you to remember and apply that truth. These notebooks will often prove to be a treasured possession to you and your children.

3. *Study reading.* Study reading may originate with, be related to, and be built upon your survey Bible reading. But in study reading you will dig deeper into the text, and you will read a text multiple times, ask the text certain key questions, use Bible study tools, and take careful notes. Study reading may focus on certain books, themes, words, doctrines, or characters in the Bible. Once again, you want to keep your notes in a notebook where they can be referenced again.

THREE TYPES OF READING

1. Devotional

2. Survey

3. Study

There will often be overlap in these various forms of reading. For example, your devotional reading may prompt you to look at a particular theme or word in other passages of the Bible. Your survey reading or study reading will often lead to devotional moments when you just want to allow God to speak to you in your innermost being. When you are prompted by the Spirit, stop and worship. Be flexible, and always approach the Bible with the anticipation that God will speak to you through His Word. Ask the Holy Spirit to be your guide and interpreter.

DEVELOP CONSISTENCY IN YOUR READING

The greatest challenge for most people when they begin a new discipline is that of developing consistency. Fitness centers prepare for a veritable onslaught of people to purchase memberships after the holidays. The purchase may be part of a New Year's resolution to lose weight or get in shape. Those who track such trivia tell me that most of those who begin with a flurry of activity often drop out within months. Discipline is the key to consistency, and consistency is the key to developing new healthy habits. Be *persistent* until you are *consistent*! No other habit that you develop will bring greater rewards than the habit of regular, effective, Bible study.

DISCIPLINE IS THE KEY TO CONSISTENCY.

Don't be deterred if you have attempted to develop a productive Bible study time before and failed. Simply confess your failure, and ask the Holy Spirit to give you the will-power to develop consistency. You can succeed this time. We are going to look at some tools that will make Bible study fun and productive. After all, mining for and discovering gold ought to be a rather exciting pastime. Until you decide that your spiritual development is worth regular study, you will likely remain a stunted, unproductive, and unfulfilled believer. Don't despair; you *can* do this and the results will be well worth it.

Make a firm commitment. Most major breakthroughs in life begin with a firm commitment that one considers to be nonnegotiable. Perhaps you have heard from your pastor the quip, "No Bible, no breakfast." Tim LaHaye, a prolific author, indicated that he first heard this phrase from a missionary he admired greatly. He had asked the missionary what was the secret to his spiritual success and effective ministry. After learning and applying this commitment, Tim shared the idea with players from the San Diego Chargers football team.[1] For many of them it was a life-changing commitment.

A simple commitment such as "No Bible, no breakfast" is a good way to remind yourself of the importance of spending time with God early in the morning. I realize you may do your more detailed Bible study later when you have more time, but it is a good practice to begin with brief devotional reading, as it sets the pattern for the day, and it ensures that you feed the soul before you feed the body. This commitment may remind you of several verses from chapter 1 that speak about the Word being like food, even like sweet honey. Here's how Job described his commitment: "I have not departed from the command of His lips; / I have treasured the words of His mouth more than my necessary food" (Job 23:12).

☐ "No Bible, no breakfast!"

Signed _____

Date _____

Have a place and time for study. The kitchen or dining room is the place we normally eat. It is interesting that merely walking into the kitchen can make you hungry. It may prompt the question, what are we eating? You have a set place for eating because the necessary implements for preserving and preparing food are there. In the same manner, you need a place where you do your Bible study. Some people prefer a comfortable chair with a side table where they keep their Bible study books. Others prefer a desk or table where they can spread out their tools. I prefer a surface where I can lay my Bible, my notebook or computer, pens or markers, and whatever Bible study tools I might need on a particular day. You will need to find your own best place and put the tools necessary for preparing your spiritual food ready at hand. Think about a place where you will experience the fewest distractions as you study.

When possible, it is helpful to have a regular time for reading or study. You might want to have a short devotional reading in the morning, a regular Bible study time at another time during the day, and then do a little survey reading before you go to bed. I do much of my survey reading by listening to entire chapters of the Bible. There are many fine, free resources that will allow you to listen to your Bible on your phone, tablet, or other electronic device. You can listen while you are preparing for bed, doing housework, working out, and so on. Be creative, but be consistent. If you miss your regular time, try to find time to make it up. Begin with a manageable time period and lengthen it when possible. You can also use bits of time to your advantage. Listen to a recording of the Bible while driving; take your Bible or electronic version of your Bible with you and read while waiting for an appointment; take Scripture memory cards with you. Warning: don't get so hung up on the time and place or the routine of Bible study that you forget that your goal is to meet with God.

YOUVERSION AND BIBLE.IS

ARE TWO FREE APPS THAT READ TO

YOU FROM MULTIPLE TRANSLATIONS

Read with anticipation. Have you ever rushed through your Bible reading without really understanding or remembering what you read? God desires to meet with us as we open His love letter. If we are not careful we can develop such a set routine for our reading that we rush through without expecting to hear from Him. For this reason, I encourage you to have your notebook beside you and your pen in your hand. When you have a pen in hand your brain is more likely to be engaged! Recording your insights will also help you to remember them. If you prefer to record your conversation with God on your computer, then have it on and ready. The goal is to find God's gold, not to dig as many holes as possible. Don't measure success by how many chapters you read, or the length of time you read, but by the quality of the time you spend with the Creator.

READING IN CONTEXT

The Bible is unique in many ways. It is actually a library of sixty-six books written by forty authors over a span of nearly fifteen hundred years. The authors include kings, shepherds, a tax collector, a fisherman, a Gentile physician, and a Pharisee turned missionary. Their diversity, reflected in their educational levels and socioeconomic lifestyles, is evident in their writings. These authors employed virtually every known literary form as they communicated God's truth. Yet the Bible has a harmonious, continuous, and complete story that flows from creation to the glorious return of Christ.

THE BIBLE HAS A HARMONIOUS,
CONTINUOUS, AND COMPLETE STORY
THAT FLOWS FROM CREATION TO THE
GLORIOUS RETURN OF CHRIST.

As we read the Bible, it is helpful to read various portions with due attention to context. *Context* is the circumstances that form the setting for a passage of Scripture by which that passage of Scripture can be rightly understood.[2] We will begin by looking at four kinds of context and then proceed by discussing how to read the various sections of the Bible with greater understanding.

Historical Context

Very simply the historical context refers to the events that were occurring at the time of the writing. These events may be recorded in the book itself or in other biblical and non-biblical accounts from the same period. When we spend time discovering the context for a passage of Scripture, we will have a clearer understanding of the Bible. It stands to reason that part of understanding the historical context requires that we pinpoint where the writing occurred in the larger story of the Bible. Understanding the historical context will keep us from lifting a passage out of its historical anchor and reading into the passage what it was never intended to convey.

Always look at the book you are reading for historical clues that are often readily available. For example, the Prophets will frequently tell you what king was on the throne at the time the author was writing. You can then look at a concordance, which contains an alphabetical list of words, and find other references to a certain king so you can look up those passages. Often you will find those kings in 1 and 2 Kings and 1 and 2 Chronicles. When you read the Gospels, it is often helpful to compare what you are reading in one gospel to the same story in another gospel.

HISTORICAL CONTEXT REFERS TO THE EVENTS THAT WERE OCCURRING AT THE TIME OF THE WRITING.

Most study Bibles will have cross-references in a center column, at the end of a verse, or in a footnote to help with this task. When you read Paul's writings, it is helpful to read the Acts account that corresponds with the founding of the church in question. For example, if I am reading 1 Corinthians, I will also want to read Acts 17–18. Acts 17 gives important insight into Paul's travels just prior to his visit to Corinth, and Acts 18 provides the story of the founding of the church.

Cultural Context

Understanding the cultural context will allow us to grasp the attitudes and patterns of behavior or expressions of a passage. Each culture had values and patterns of behavior that impacted interaction and communication in those cultures.

UNDERSTANDING THE CULTURAL CONTEXT WILL ALLOW US TO GRASP THE ATTITUDES AND PATTERNS OF BEHAVIOR OR EXPRESSIONS OF A PASSAGE.

When I was president of Southwestern Seminary I had to learn how to interact appropriately in different cultural contexts. Our Korean students had a profound respect for those in authority and would slightly bow as they shook hands. In preparation for my trip to Korea, I sought advice on what was appropriate behavior in their culture. This made my trip to Korea a success but did little to prepare me for dealing with *real* cowboys. Early in my presidency I made a cultural faux pas. I was walking down the hall and spied a Hoss-Cartwright-style 10-gallon hat on the desk of one of our professors. I quickly stepped through the door and placed the hat on my own head. I thought everyone would enjoy a laugh as the hat swallowed my head. Somewhat quickly, and quite abruptly, a "genuine cowboy" took his hat back without so much as a smile. Later, this professor told me that you never touch another man's hat.

Some examples of cultural details that would impact the way we read and understand the Bible include such matters as worship practices during the time of Jesus, the beliefs and practices of a Pharisee or Sadducee, the wearing of one's hair or use of head coverings (1 Cor. 11:4–6), behavior at a wedding or funeral, eating practices, attitudes toward giving, and existing prejudices.

You will begin to understand many of these cultural clues as you read the Bible. However there are several tools that you can consult to ensure that you understand a text in the light of its cultural context. Many study Bibles will include such details in the study notes. Most commentaries will offer insight about the cultural context of a passage, and a good Bible dictionary is an invaluable tool as well. You can look up topics such as "ablutions," "grief and mourning," "greeting," and "Jews in the New Testament" in a Bible dictionary. The list is countless, and the results will provide endless nuggets of gold.

Literary Context

Now we consider how a passage fits and/or functions in a book, a group of books, or the Bible as a whole. It also means that we must read a particular book with an awareness of the type of literature we are reading. For example, we would read the Poetical Books differently than we read the Historical Books. We read Paul differently than we read a Gospel, since we know he is addressing a particular church in a particular area. We will look at literary types in greater detail later in this chapter.

A passage that illustrates the importance of both cultural and literary context is found in 1 Corinthians 11 where Paul gave permission for women to pray and prophesy if they did so with their heads covered (v. 5). He made it clear that a contentious woman had no authority to teach, and that the churches had no other practice (v. 16). Later, in 1 Corinthians 14:34–36, Paul seemed to restrict women from any speech within the church. Clearly both passages must be interpreted with a sense of both their literary and cultural contexts. We would want first to understand the cultural issue of the head covering, and second, we would want to understand the literary context of each passage since it is impossible for these two passages by the hand of the same author, and inspired by the Holy Spirit, to contradict one another. I told you Bible study was exciting and that you would find gold.

Theological Context

We must always be careful to ask how a text and its topic fit into the various theological themes in the Bible. Andreas Kostenberger defines theological context as follows: "We are not just looking for the historical facts but also asking questions about what stories, or practices, or institutions tell us about God, or about ourselves as human beings, or the world in which we live. We also are asking about the development of those ideas over time, as God revealed truth progressively in the development of the biblical story."[3]

While the idea of studying theology is intimidating to some and irrelevant to others in the modern-day church, nothing could be further from the truth. *Theology* simply means "a word about God," and all of us need a clear and accurate word about God. Right theology will ensure that we think correctly about God, ourselves, our relationships, and the broader world in which we live. Right thinking is the nonnegotiable foundation for right behavior. Thus theology is a very practical discipline because it helps us to live in harmony with God's purpose for our lives.

Much of Paul's corrective teaching in the letter we call 1 Corinthians is firmly rooted in theological truth. For example, Paul dealt with the issue of sexual immorality by reminding the people that their body is the temple of the Holy Spirit who was in them (6:19). He based his teaching about sexual purity on the doctrine of redemption: "For you have been bought with a price: therefore glorify God in your body"

(6:20). Understanding the theological context of a particular passage will add both understanding and application.

FOUR CONTEXTS TO CONSIDER

- Historical
- Cultural
- Literary
- Theological

READING AND UNDERSTANDING THE LIBRARY OF BOOKS

As we have already seen, our great library of books contains several different contexts and several different types of books. In the Old Testament we have the historical narratives or stories, the Law and the Prophets, and the books of poetry, which include Psalms. In the New Testament we have the Gospels or stories, and contained therein, we have the teaching of Jesus (many of which are parables). Acts is the second volume of Luke's writing and provides a historical narrative of the birth and spread of the church. Further we have the Pauline and General Letters and the book of Revelation.

The Old Testament

Some people avoid the Old Testament because they think it is too difficult to understand or too dated to have any contemporary significance. They find its length, strange laws and customs, and minute attention to detail a bit much to tackle. Yet the Old Testament is as much God's Word as is

the New Testament, and therefore the reading and understanding of it is vital to our understanding of the character
and activity of God. Further, it is impossible to understand
the New Testament without having an appropriate understanding of the Old. When Jesus or Paul spoke about understanding and obeying "the Scriptures" they were referring
to the Old Testament since the New Testament did not yet
exist. As you begin to dig into the Old Testament, you will
find it a rich treasure trove and an exciting drama of God's
progressive revelation of Himself.

Let's quickly review the divisions of the Old Testament from our chart in chapter 2. The first five books of
the Old Testament are referred to as the Torah (or Pentateuch). These books contain the story of the beginning of
the world and Israel as a nation. The Historical Books begin
with Joshua and conclude with Esther. They recount the history of Israel from the time they finally entered the promised land, were taken into captivity, and began the return to
the land. The Poetical Books include Job, Psalms, Proverbs,
Ecclesiastes, and Song of Solomon. The final category is the
Prophets, divided between the Major and Minor Prophets.
Let's take a quick look at how to read various books found
in these divisions.

THE DIVISIONS OF THE OLD TESTAMENT

- Pentateuch
- Historical Books
- Poetical Books
- Major Prophets
- Minor Prophets

READING THE STORIES

When we speak of the stories of the Old Testament, we are not referring to fictional events such as those in a novel or children's book. Tragically we often teach these historical narratives in church in a manner that makes them appear to be moralistic stories in the same vein as fairy tales. Nothing could be further from the truth. These are historical and biographical accounts of events that occurred in the real world.

When I first returned from Cambridge, I taught an Old Testament survey course at a small school in North Carolina. Since it was a Baptist school our students were required to take a couple of Bible courses. Many of the students approached them with indifference if not outright hostility. The non-Christians didn't see why they needed to take a course on the Bible. Some of the Christians were indifferent because they saw the course as a repeat of Sunday school. One particularly bright student gave every visual clue of absolute boredom. One day, as I was lecturing on one of the kings of Israel, he sat straight up and paid close attention. His body language indicated he was tuned in to what I was saying. I dismissed class a few minutes early and pulled him aside to ask him what had gotten his attention. He responded that when I spoke of the biblical king, I also placed his ministry in the historical context of a certain pagan king. He then told me that they had studied about the reign of this pagan king in his "real history" class. What had shocked him was that the Bible was "real history" and not just "Sunday school history." We have sometimes treated the stories of the Old Testament as if they occurred in a parallel universe such as C. S. Lewis's "Narnia," where beavers talk and Lions die for you. Yes, these real stories are included in God's love letter for our benefit.

As you read the stories ask yourself these questions:

1. What is the purpose of this story?

2. What characteristics of God are portrayed?

3. What characteristics of man are portrayed?

4. What does God value?

5. What is God's agenda?

You should always ask the newspaper reporter's questions—who, what, when, where, why, and how. When reading the Bible it is always appropriate and important to ask, so what. That is, what does God want me to learn from this story?

When you are reading, keep in mind that God is the author and the central character of the Bible. He is the hero of every story in the Bible. God took the initiative to reveal Himself to humans, and therefore every story adds to our understanding of Him. At the same time, the stories are about men and women with whom God desired to have an intimate and eternal relationship. Therefore we discover nuggets of gold as we look closely at the human characters in the stories. Why were they chosen? Why did they fail or succeed? The stories often have at their core the honest struggle of people to trust God with the details of their lives. Isn't this true about all of us? We struggle to live by faith. We struggle with God's call to service, arguing as Moses did that we are unworthy. These stories have much to teach us about our journey with God.

READING THE LAW AND THE PROPHETS

If you have ever attempted to read the Bible through, you may have bogged down in Leviticus. You wonder what do all the hundreds of laws God gave to the Hebrew people about food, cleanliness, and other assorted matters have to do with us today? They may seem like so many trivia if we forget that God gave them to His ancient people to allow them to walk in relationship with Him in their time and culture. We have to read them according to God's intended purpose. In the same way, the historical references and puzzling messages of the prophets can be confusing to the modern-day reader without due attention to the historical context.

Much of the content of the first five books of the Bible (the Torah or Pentateuch) is made up of the historical stories and the laws God gave to the people of Israel. The laws actually teach us much about God's character and His purpose in the world. That's right, the Bible is about Him. The laws addressed the problem of sin and offered a temporary solution for cleansing in anticipation of the ultimate forgiveness of sin and redemption of humanity that Jesus would bring.

> THE LAWS TEACH US MUCH ABOUT GOD'S CHARACTER AND HIS PURPOSE IN THE WORLD.

When we ask how the laws fit into the bigger story of the Old Testament, we must first place them in their historical context. God gave the law to prepare Israel to enter the promised land and to live as the people of a holy God in the midst of a pagan people. For example, when God gave laws about crossbreeding animals or sowing fields with two kinds of seeds or putting two kinds of material on one garment (Lev. 19:19), He was giving Israel a graphic picture of separation from the pagan practices around them. While specific laws may seem dated to the modern-day reader, the principles behind them remain true for God's people today.

This naturally leads to the question of how the law is relevant in our time. Believers are no longer under the Mosaic covenant. George Guthrie says, "Although the books of the law are still Scripture—God's infallible Word to us—they are no longer law for us. Therefore, we should read and apply the Old Testament not as legally binding laws, but as embodying principles we should glean and obey. What do the laws teach us about God? What do they teach us about human nature? What guidelines do we find that can help us live for the Lord in the world today?"[4]

When we hear the word *prophet* we tend to think of the word *prediction*. While certain Old Testament prophets did speak of future events, the prophets were more than spiritual forecasters. The prophets were real people who spoke a critical message in Jewish history to a unique segment of God's people. There are sixteen books of prophecy in total—four major and twelve minor—the difference being length, not importance. These sixteen books were written between 800 and 400 BC in four distinct phases of the history of God's people.

- The eighth-century prophets: Jonah, Isaiah, Micah, Hosea, and Amos
- The rise of the Babylonian Empire: Jeremiah, Nahum, Zephaniah, Obadiah, Joel, and Habakkuk
- The exile: Ezekiel and Daniel
- After the exile: Haggai, Zechariah, and Malachi

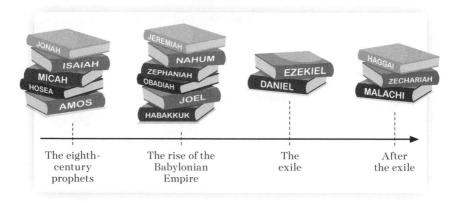

| The eighth-
century
prophets | The rise of the
Babylonian
Empire | The
exile | After
the exile |

Relevant questions to ask as you read the prophets in their historical context include who was the king at the time, was the prophet writing to the Northern Kingdom or the Southern Kingdom, what was the situation at the time, and were the people obeying or disobeying God. Most of these answers can be found in the text, but a commentary or Bible dictionary can help with these questions.

In most cases the prophets were like many modern-day preachers—they had three main points: (1) the call to be faithful to the covenant in their behavior, often by carrying out justice for the poor and disadvantaged; (2) the promise of judgment if repentance did not occur; and (3) hope for the future, many times expressed in terms of a remnant that would be saved. Often the hope points to a messianic coming and kingdom.

Again, we cannot leave our study of any prophet without asking the final question, what do these messages have to do with me? The simple answer is *everything*. In each message we see God at work in His world in spite of the rebellion of man. We see His persistent and consistent compassion in seeking us out, even in our rebellion. We can see the consequences of rebellion and the glorious future for those who return to Him.

READING THE POETICAL BOOKS

The book of Psalms consists of the songs of the Old Testament, and like songs of any generation, they give expression to man's thoughts and feelings. In the case of the Old Testament songs, they help us reflect on God and life. David wrote seventy-three, or nearly half of them, and the rest were written by various individuals over the thousand-year period between Moses and the time of exile in Babylon. Some psalms are corporate—expressing worship or recounting God's redemptive intervention—while others are personal and express a variety of emotions, including love, anger, fear, surprise, disappointment, and hope. God created us as emotional beings, and He allows us to express our emotions even when some are self-centered and less than righteous.

GOD CREATED US AS EMOTIONAL BEINGS, AND HE ALLOWS US TO EXPRESS OUR EMOTIONS.

As we read a psalm, we need to ask first about its purpose. Many were written for corporate worship and were thus intended to be used in a large group setting. Some will begin with a note such as "For the choir director; on stringed instruments." Even some of the psalms that express personal emotions were used in a corporate worship context. Once we understand the purpose of a psalm, we should ask how we need to respond.

The authors of the psalms often used word pictures and figurative language. The beloved Psalm 23 is a great example of the use of word pictures. To fully understand this psalm it is helpful to know something about the work of a shepherd in biblical days. With that in mind we would need to know that green pastures represent rest and provision, and the terms *rod* and *staff* speak to protection and guidance. The various psalmists used poetic language that is often very picturesque. A common poetic device is parallelism which means that two lines of the poetry are closely related, the second either repeating something similar to the first or contrasting with it. For example, "I cry aloud with my voice to the LORD, / I make supplication with my voice to the LORD" (142:1).

As you read Psalms you will want to ask about its original intent and seek to find its use in Israel's life. But further you will want to allow the psalms to guide you in prayer and worship. As you read a psalm, make it your prayer. You can do so by reading it the way it is written or you can put your prayer in your own words.

Proverbs and Ecclesiastes are the most recognizable of the Wisdom Books in the Old Testament. Wisdom literature often includes pithy sayings that require us to apply truth gained from experience to our own lives. Gordon Fee and Douglas Stuart give rules which are helpful in reading wisdom literature, particularly the proverbs. I am abbreviating their material, and you would profit from reading the entire chapter of their book:

1. They are often figurative, pointing beyond themselves.

2. They are intensely practical, not theoretically theological.

3. They are worded to be memorable, not technically precise.

4. They strongly reflect ancient culture.

5. They are not guarantees from God, but poetic guidelines for good behavior.

6. They use various literary techniques, such as exaggeration to make their point.

7. They give good advice but are not exhaustive in their coverage.

8. Wrongly used, they might suggest a crass, materialistic lifestyle. Rightly used, they provide practical advice for daily living.[5]

The New Testament

THE DIVISIONS OF THE NEW TESTAMENT

- Gospels and Acts
- Pauline Epistles
- General Epistles
- Prophecy

READING THE STORIES

Nearly 60 percent of the New Testament is presented in story form, and the majority of the stories are found in the four gospels and the book of Acts. To understand any biblical story we must remember that it must first be understood in the light of the culture of its time. After we understand the story in the light of its original culture we are prepared to apply the story.

For example, you might wonder why the Pharisees were so upset when Jesus ate with tax collectors (cf. Matt. 9:9–13). Many righteous Jews lived by regulations which would prevent them from being ceremonially defiled at meals. The Pharisees thought that separation from unclean sinners was necessary to maintain righteousness. Further, sharing a meal with someone indicated social equality. Now do you see why the Pharisees were so offended by Jesus' actions? Do you see what Jesus was doing? He was demonstrating God's grace and love for everyone.

Three of the gospels—Matthew, Mark, and Luke—are called the *Synoptic* ("to see together") Gospels because they tell the story of Jesus from beginning to end (chronologically), allowing Jesus' story to unfold gradually. The gospel of John, however, is more theological and begins with Jesus in heaven before time began. John structured the story around seven great sign events that clearly demonstrated who Jesus is. Although all the gospels tell the story of Jesus, each has different emphases, themes, and storytelling techniques. For example, Luke the Gentile physician was intrigued by the various healing miracles, and he included stories about women and those considered outcasts. Matthew's gospel has more of the teaching sections, and Mark's gospel focuses on Jesus' activity.

The gospel writers presented their message through the materials they selected to include and the order in which they organized the material. Under the direction of the Holy Spirit, their selection of material was related to their purpose in writing. For example, Matthew wanted to demonstrate to the Jews that Jesus is the promised Messiah. For that reason his genealogy (ch. 1) and his use of Old Testament prophecy are unique. The fact that God gave us four different gospels reaffirms His desire to give us a complete picture, providing four different witnesses to add detail and clarity to the story. Acts is volume 2 of Luke's narrative and provides a historical picture of what Jesus continued to do through the planting of His church by the empowering of the Holy Spirit (Acts 1:1).

As in the stories of the Old Testament, God is still the central character and hero of each story, but in the New Testament God the Son is clearly the main character. So in each story we should first ask, what does this story tell me about Jesus? We must then ask how we are to respond.

A COMMON THEME OF JESUS' TEACHING IS THE KINGDOM OF GOD.

READING THE TEACHINGS OF JESUS

The teachings of Jesus are found in the four gospels, but because of their importance, we must consider them as a unique category. However please remember that the rest of the Bible is equally as authoritative as Jesus' teaching, since the Holy Spirit is the author of all Scripture. Jesus taught His lessons in real-life situations that we can discover as we read the Gospels. By paying attention to the context, the methods, and themes of His teaching, these lessons will become even more clear, rich, and life-changing.

Sometimes the teachings are grouped by a common theme. It is possible that Jesus presented His teachings multiple times and in a variety of settings. At times we will note that a gospel writer grouped certain stories thematically. In other instances it seems obvious that Jesus Himself put together various story illustrations to make a main theme even clearer.

A common theme of Jesus' teaching is the kingdom of God. Matthew's gospel tells us that following His temptation in the wilderness, Jesus began to preach about the kingdom (4:17). Much of the interest in the kingdom and the anointed King (Messiah) in Jesus' day was related to political freedom from Roman dominion. It is no wonder that His announcement concerning the arrival of God's kingdom caught everyone's attention. While it is clear that Jesus knew that He was the anointed King (Matt. 16:16–17), He spoke of a kingdom that is eternal in nature and offers spiritual freedom to all who will turn from their sin and enter into a relationship with God through Him. Jesus' teachings about the kingdom are as radical in our day as they were in the first century. They challenge us to live with allegiance to the one true King in a world that is in the process of decay and destruction.

Jesus, the master Teacher, used a variety of methods that included parables, speeches, sermons, proverbs, riddles, drama, object lessons, Old Testament quotations, dialogue, hyperbole, metaphor, and rhetorical questions. The greatest challenge most readers face is that of reading a familiar story or parable with fresh eyes and an open heart.

Because Jesus taught so often in parables, it is important that we give them special attention. George Guthrie defines a parable as "a creative story told to illustrate a spiritual truth."[6] Craig Blomberg suggests several key principles to keep in mind as we read the parables. He indicates that the stories employ a few key characters to represent God and various ways of responding to Him and His kingdom. In about two-thirds of the parables there will be a master figure (king, father, landlord, etc.) whose actions in some way mirror God's actions. We also find pairs such as a good son and a wicked son. Often the son or servant who turns out to be good is not what we might have expected in the beginning.[7]

As we read and study the teachings of Jesus, keep in mind that Jesus' goal was to call people to Himself and shape disciples to be fit for the kingdom of God. While Bible study is a fascinating venture, God's purpose is to transform the reader, not simply inform him.

READING THE LETTERS

We have mentioned frequently the necessity of understanding the historical context of a passage, and in reading the Letters this is even more critical. God saw fit to give us twenty of the twenty-seven books in the New Testament in the form of letters. We must first understand the historical occasion that prompted the writing of a particular letter. The best clues are contained in the letters themselves. In the case of the Pauline Letters, Acts will also add invaluable material.

Each letter was written to address specific situations in a particular church or group of churches. The more we can learn about the writer, the people being addressed, and the situation that prompted the letter, the greater will be our understanding of the timeless principles of the letter. I always recommend that you attempt to get most of your clues for understanding the historical situation from the letter itself. This may require multiple readings, but it will prove to be well worth the investment. If necessary, you can consult a commentary to check or supplement your understanding.

Most New Testament letters will follow a similar structure, which includes a greeting from the author to the recipient, a word of thanksgiving or blessing, an opening introduction, the body of the letter, and a closing or benediction. The opening section is always critical, and it is there the author will often provide most of the clues to understanding a letter. For example, if you read 1 Corinthians 1: 1–17 you will find a wealth of information beyond the writer and recipient. You will notice the theme of "grace" and emphasis on abundance (words such as "everything" and "all" predominate), spiritual gifts, and divisions in the church.

READING REVELATION

The book of Revelation presents us with special challenges and blessings (1:3). As you read it, always remember you must first read it in light of the original audience. We often engage in end-time speculation without asking first what the passage said and meant to its first-century audience. Revelation belongs to a class of literature referred to as *apocalyptic*. In a series of visions, God gave John the ability to see what was going on behind world events. For this reason, we must pay close attention to the use of symbols and how John, the author, interpreted those symbols.

APOCALYPTIC IS DERIVED FROM A GREEK WORD WHICH MEANS "TO UNCOVER." IT IS THE OPENING WORD OF THE BOOK OF REVELATION AND SIGNIFIES IT IS AN UNVEILING BY GOD. APOCALYPTIC LITERATURE EMPLOYS HIGHLY SYMBOLIC LANGUAGE.

Revelation was written during a time of severe persecution and thus used coded language, especially symbols, to communicate truth. In addition to revealing future events, it conveys a message of encouragement for believers as they struggle against evil in the world. Don't try to find a precise historical chronology; rather focus on grasping the primary message of each vision. Above all, approach the text prayerfully and humbly. Scripture should unite believers and not divide them. Beware of any interpretation that claims to be the final and perfect interpretation of the book of Revelation. Take encouragement that this book demonstrates that whatever may be the circumstances of your life or our world, God is in ultimate and total control.

TOOLS FOR THE SERIOUS MINER

Let me return to the original question with which we began our study. What if you discovered that there was a pure vein of gold in your back yard? No doubt you would be passionate to unearth it. Clearly one of your first steps would be to find out all you could about gold and the process of mining it. That is precisely what we have been doing in these first three chapters. As we have progressed we have seen that some nuggets of gold can be found readily, but others require a little more digging. So the serious miner is going to purchase the tools necessary for unearthing the gold. Truth is, most of us would probably head out quickly to purchase a pick and shovel so we could dig down to find the hidden treasure. It wouldn't be long before we were headed to the farm equipment store for a backhoe. We would gladly make the purchase knowing that the results would be well worth the expenditure.

There are tools that every serious Bible student needs to have. The good news is that most of these are very affordable, and many are free online. Refer to Appendix B for a simple list of essential tools to get you started in finding gold. I am including both those in book form, computer software, and online resources. There are advantages to all of them. Many people enjoy the process of looking through and marking their own book. The computer tools have the advantage of speed. You can access word studies very quickly through the online tools.

MINE THE GOLD

1. Begin today to build your gold mining tool kit.

2. Read the first chapter of each of the four gospels and note the differences.

3. As time allows, read a chapter from one of the biblical books in each category mentioned in this chapter.

CHAPTER 4

Discovering the Plain
Meaning of the Text

At this point you may be feeling a bit like a prospector kneeling beside a stream with pan in hand, revealing lots of gold dust and a few sizeable nuggets. Your hard work has paid rich dividends, but you know there must be more gold just beneath the surface. Your appetite has been whetted, and you want to dig down to find the vein of gold that yielded the dust and nuggets you have discovered thus far.

In chapter 1, our first panning experience, we found gold dust as we discovered the benefit of studying God's Word and the attitudes that are necessary for true comprehension. In chapter 2, our second pan, we found numerous nuggets as we looked at six essential truths about the Bible, how it is organized, and the big picture that flows from Genesis to Revelation. As we dipped our pan for a third time in chapter 3 we found nuggets that help us to read the Bible more effectively. We discussed three different types of Bible reading, with each of them providing riches in very different ways. We also found that for the larger nuggets of gold we need to be aware of the historical, cultural, literary, and theological contexts of what we are reading. After all, we have a library of sixty-six books that contain rich diversity in the material.

Now we are ready to dig down and search for the vein of pure gold that has already yielded so much with our panning method. As we begin the digging process the work may be a bit more challenging, but the results will be well worth it. The joy is found not only in the discovery but also in the actual process of digging. Let the fun begin!

MAKING SENSE OF ALL YOU READ

Now let's talk about the process of interpreting the Bible. Before you opt out, thinking this is a task for professors and pastors, let me assure you that you can do this and that you will actually enjoy learning how to understand all you are reading. Some people think interpretation is unnecessary since all one needs to do is read the Bible and obey it. While I heartily agree we must read and obey the Bible, I also insist that proper interpretation is the key to reading with the understanding that ultimately leads to obedience.

Gordon Fee and Douglas Stuart begin their excellent book *How to Read the Bible for All Its Worth* with a chapter entitled "The Need to Interpret." They write:

> Because the Bible is God's Word, it has *eternal relevance;* it speaks to all mankind, in every age and in every culture. Because it is God's Word, we must listen—and obey. But because God chose to speak His Word through *human words in history,* every book in the Bible also has *historical particularity;* each document is conditioned by the language, time, and culture in which it was originally written (and in some cases also by the oral history it had before it was written down). Interpretation of the Bible is demanded by the "tension'" that exists between its *eternal relevance* and its *historical particularity.*[1]

Truth is, we can't read the Bible without interpreting it. When we read the Bible we bring to the text our life experiences, culture, understanding of words and ideas, and messages or lessons that we have heard from others. For example, when we read Paul's letters to the early churches, we often have in mind churches we have seen or visited. Thus we may think of Paul's instructions about taking the Lord's Supper in 1 Corinthians 11 a bit unusual because we have in mind a traditional sanctuary or fellowship hall. This inadvertent mind-set actually colors our understanding or interpretation of the text. We may immediately think of a sermon we have heard on the text, and thus we carry that interpretation with us to the text without consciously thinking about it.

Everyone who works with the biblical text will become involved in interpretation. Persons who work in Bible translation are required to make choices regarding meanings of words in context, and those choices may impact your understanding of a text. For example, when you read 1 Corinthians 14:2 most translations use language that suggests that what is occurring in Corinth is "speaking in tongues" or the use of "unintelligible prayer language." The New American Standard Bible, which is a very literal translation, says, "For one who speaks in a tongue." The Holman Christian Standard Bible, however, speaks of human language, "For the person who speaks in another language," and not an unintelligible prayer language. In this case, the translators have become interpreters, and their interpretation may affect your reading and understanding of this particular verse and the entire fourteenth chapter.

Every reader is an interpreter, and therefore our goal is to be the best interpreters possible. The antidote to bad interpretation is not *no* interpretation but *correct* interpretation. In most cases correct interpretation is the plain meaning of the text. Ask this question of everything you read: does it make sense of the text in its context, and does it stand in harmony with the rest of Scripture? The Bible does not contradict itself, and the Holy Spirit inspired the authors to write what they meant in a straightforward fashion. However, they spoke in language and idioms that were common to their day, and these must then be interpreted.

IN MOST CASES CORRECT INTERPRETATION IS THE PLAIN MEANING OF THE TEXT. ASK THIS QUESTION: DOES IT MAKE SENSE OF THE TEXT IN ITS CONTEXT, AND DOES IT STAND IN HARMONY WITH THE REST OF SCRIPTURE?

The primary reason we must be careful to interpret Scripture accurately is that we are commanded to do so: "Be diligent to present yourself approved to God as a workman who does not need to be ashamed, accurately handling the word of truth" (2 Tim. 2:15). While Paul originally gave this command to young Timothy, it applies to everyone who wants to mine the pure gold found in God's Word.

THE BIBLE IS GOD'S WORD SPOKEN THROUGH REAL PEOPLE IN REAL HISTORY

This brings us to the tension between *historical particularity* and *eternal relevance*. Let's think for a minute about the matter of the historical particularity as it relates to what you are reading.

Determine each book's historical setting. Each book was written at a particular time to a particular people with a unique culture and language. Understanding the historical. setting will help us to understand its original message and apply that truth to our lives today.

Obviously the historical context of the book of Amos and that of Luke will be considerably different. They wrote at different times and with different audiences in mind. The documents themselves will often provide important clues that will help us to determine answers to some of the questions about historical particularity. For example, Amos 1:1 tells us that Amos "was among the sheepherders from Tekoa" who prophesied during the "days of Uzziah king of Judah, and in the days of Jeroboam." It is often helpful to consult a commentary or Bible dictionary to help you answer some questions. If you look up "Tekoa" in the *Holman Bible Dictionary*, you will find that it means "place of setting up a tent" and that it is a city in the highlands of Judah six miles south of Bethlehem. You could also look up "Uzziah" in a Bible dictionary, or you could look in a concordance and find other biblical references to him. Luke, on the other hand, was a Gentile physician who was not an eyewitness but who interviewed eyewitnesses so that he could tell the story of Jesus accurately and in consecutive order (Luke 1:1–4). Luke provides us with information about himself and how he collected and organized his material. It is always important to read a book with a clear understanding of its historical setting.

EACH BOOK WAS WRITTEN AT A PARTICULAR TIME TO A PARTICULAR PEOPLE.

Determine the time and culture of the author. Look at issues such as geography, topography, and political climate of the time of the author and recipients. This is often more of a challenge with Old Testament books since they cover such a large time period. If you can't find a sufficient number of clues in the text, consult a commentary or Bible dictionary. The time period of New Testament books is more limited beginning around AD 48 or 49 with the writing of Galatians and concluding in the mid-90s with the writing of Revelation. You can obtain some clues about the political climate through reading the various books, but once again, good commentaries will help you understand the political climate. Most Bibles have a limited number of maps in the back that are related to both the Old and New Testaments. The map section will help you to understand some information about relative location. For additional information you will need to purchase a larger Bible atlas.

Determine the occasion and purpose of each book. In some cases the author will clearly state his purpose for writing, and in others you may have to read the material several times to get a sense of the purpose. We have already noticed that Luke indicated he was putting his material in consecutive order, "So that you may know the exact truth about the things you have been taught" (Luke 1:4). When you read John's gospel you will find a clear indication of his purpose in chapter 20: "But these have been written so that you may believe that Jesus is the Christ, the Son of God; and that believing you may have life in His name" (v. 31). Further, he indicated that he selected certain stories among many that could have been told (21:25). If you are looking for the occasion of a book such as 1 Corinthians, it is helpful to read the Acts account of the founding of the church at Corinth (18:1–17) and then read 1 Corinthians several times. As you are reading 1 Corinthians you will notice that Paul had heard from Chloe's people that there were quarrels in the church (1:11). If you continue reading, chapter 7 tells that the

YOU MAY HAVE TO READ THE MATERIAL SEVERAL TIMES TO GET A SENSE OF THE AUTHOR'S PURPOSE.

Corinthians wrote to Paul asking for clarification or additional information about matters which he must have taught them in person: "Now concerning the things about which you wrote, it is good for a man not to touch a woman" (v. 1). Paul repeated the phrase "now concerning" again in 8:1, 12:1, and 16:1. Thus we can conclude that Paul was writing to deal with new issues that had emerged since his departure and areas of confusion that prompted the Corinthians to write to him for clarification.

Determine the literary context of every passage. Words have meaning in sentences, and those sentences have meaning in relation to preceding and succeeding sentences. Let's revisit 1 Corinthians 7 to illustrate the importance of context. When you read the first verse, you might be somewhat confused by the statement, "It is good for a man not to touch a woman." Did Paul really mean that there shouldn't be any physical or sexual contact between men and women, particularly those who are married? As you continue to read you will find that Paul spoke of the importance of sexual intimacy between a man and his wife (vv. 3–5). So obviously he was not suggesting that there be no physical contact nor was he contradicting himself. In the first verse, Paul accurately quoted a view that had been promoted by someone in Corinth—a celibate lifestyle. Paul had to correct this misunderstanding first before he could establish a more balanced view of appropriate sexual behavior. We can further illustrate the importance of being aware of the larger context by looking at 1 Corinthians 8:1: "Now concerning things sacrificed to idols, we know that we have all knowledge." Did Paul believe that Christians have all knowledge? Such a suggestion would clearly contradict 1 Corinthians 13:12 where Paul said, "Now I know in part." Further, if we look back at 8:2, we will find Paul's correction where he indicated that present knowledge is incomplete. Once again Paul actually quoted a question that includes a false premise and then brought correction. We must continually ask, what is the point, and what did the author intend to say?

Determine the actual content of the words. This means we must look at the meaning of words as used in the present text as well as other biblical texts. To find other uses of a particular word, simply consult a concordance to find other relevant passages. We also know that words can have several different meanings. For example, the word *trunk* can mean a box, a tree trunk, or a car trunk. You can only know the word's actual meaning by reading it in a sentence, which gives the context for determining the proper meaning. Further, we must always pay attention to the grammar and syntax of the sentence. Most reliable translations will often give you clues as to whether the sentence is a statement, a question, or an exclamation.

A good concordance can assist you further with the study of words in their context. Most study Bibles have concordances, but the concordances are limited because they are only a few pages in length. You can purchase a concise concordance that contains the most significant occurrences of a given word or an exhaustive concordance that contains many more entries. Most software Bible study programs will include concordances. Since concordances are normally based on a particular Bible translation, make sure that the concordance you use is based on the translation that you normally use for study.

Let's look at a simple example of the importance of the meaning of words in content and context. The Ephesian and Colossian letters were written at the same time by Paul from a Roman prison. As you read the letters you will notice that Tychicus is bringing both letters with additional information about Paul's condition (Eph. 6:21; Col. 4:7). In reading the two letters together you may notice the repetition of the word "fullness" (Eph. 1:10, 23; 3:19; 4:13; Col. 1:19; 2:9). (I am working from the New American Standard Bible which is my study Bible of preference.) If I check my concordance, I will find that this word occurs only ten times in the entire New Testament, and six of those occurrences are in these two short letters. That is a significant number, which indicates that this is a particularly important term for these letters. Both references in Colossians speak of Christ as the fullness of God. In Ephesians the first use relates to the fullness of the times (1:10) and is thus similar to Galatians 4:4. The other references in Ephesians use the term "fullness" in relationship to the church. This is an important discovery and indicates that Paul is affirming the incredible significance of the church as the earthly community designed and empowered to display God's fullness as Christ did in His incarnation.

Determine the type of literature you are reading. In chapter 3, we learned that the Bible is a treasure trove of literary types: historical narrative, poetic literature, hymns, proverbs, prophecy, gospels, letters, and apocalyptic literature. For example, much of the New Testament is made up of the Gospels and Letters or Epistles, but Revelation is an example of apocalyptic literature that employs highly symbolic language to tell of divine intervention. Poetic literature is primarily found in Psalms, but poetry can also be found in other books in the Old and New Testaments. Many translations will often indent poetic literature so that you will know when you are reading it. Further, the Bible contains hyperbole (exaggeration), figures of speech, irony, metaphors, and personification. Word pictures suggesting that the trees clap their hands (Isa. 55:12) or the stones cry out (Luke 19:40) are clearly figures of speech. The use of such figurative language does not constitute an error as some liberal scholars like to suggest. In truth, it simply reveals God's desire to impart his eternal truth in clear and understandable language.

TYPES OF LITERATURE

Letters	Proverbs
Historical narrative	Hymns
Gospels	Apocalyptic literature
Poetic literature	Prophecy

6 THINGS TO LOOK FOR AS YOU READ EACH TEXT:

- Historical particularity
- Time and culture of the author
- Occasion and purpose of the book
- Literary context of each passage
- Actual content of the words
- Type of literature being read

HELPFUL HINTS FOR DISCOVERING THE PLAIN MEANING OF THE TEXT

Watch for natural divisions in the text. As you read, notice that the text is divided into verses and often marked or indented by paragraph notation. These devices help you to see the paragraph structure of the writing. Keep in mind, however, that verse numbers and paragraph breaks were added by later translators to help us understand the text and thus should only be used as a guideline.

Pay attention to the amount of space devoted to a topic. The amount of space an author devoted to a particular topic reveals the importance of that topic in a particular book. For example, you will notice that Paul devoted three entire chapters to the discussion of spiritual gifts in 1 Corinthians 12–14. Clearly the matter of spiritual gifts was critical to the corrective teaching addressed to this young church. In Galatians Paul placed a consistent emphasis on the matter of grace and works, giving us a clue as to his intention for writing this letter.

Note the repetition of certain words, phrases, or themes. This repetition demonstrates the importance of an idea in a particular letter or book. For example, a simple reading of 1 Corinthians 13 will cause you to note a repetition of the word "love." Thus love is the focal point of this passage. If we further note that this entire chapter is in the very center of an extended discussion on spiritual gifts we see that the chapter is an important corrective for the use of spiritual gifts in the assembly.

Look for relationships in the text. Various relationships may occur in the text you are reading:

❀ **You will often find "if, then" constructions.** In Exodus 19:5 the Lord told Israel: "If you will indeed obey My voice and keep My covenant, then you shall be My own possession among all the peoples, for all the earth is Mine." In addition, most of us are familiar with the famous promise related to prayer for revival: [If] My people who are called by My name humble themselves and pray and seek My face and turn from their wicked ways, then I will hear from heaven, will forgive their sin and will heal their land (2 Chr. 7:14). God's healing of the land is contingent on His people praying, seeking His face, and turning from their wicked ways. God's activity is contingent on man's obedient response.

✸ **You will also find relationships of cause and effect.** In the parable of the talents, the master told his servant, "You were faithful with a few things, I will put you in charge of many things" (Matt. 25:21).

✸ **Another relationship is comparison and contrasts.** In the Sermon on the Mount, Jesus compared and contrasted His new teaching with what they had heard from the ancient teachers: "You have heard that the ancients were told, 'YOU SHALL NOT COMMIT MURDER' and 'Whoever commits murder shall be liable to the court.' But I say to you that everyone who is angry with his brother shall be guilty before the court; and whoever says to his brother, 'You good-for-nothing,' shall be guilty before the supreme court; and whoever says, 'You fool,' shall be guilty enough to go into the fiery hell (Matt. 5:21–22). Reading with care will make your reading more enjoyable and profitable.

Distinguish between matters that are prescriptive and those that are descriptive. An author of Scripture may be accurately describing an event that has occurred but not necessarily prescribing that event for every believer in every time period. For example, in 1 Corinthians 11 Paul accurately described the practice of women covering their heads before praying or prophesying in the assembly. The description of this first-century practice does not mean that women in every church in every generation should wear a head covering. The clear teaching of the text is that women must have the right goal and attitude when participating in worship. The contentious woman is not allowed to speak (v. 16).

Another example could be taken from John 13 where Jesus washed His disciples' feet before they partook of the Passover meal. One's understanding of the culture is helpful. Men wore sandals, and thus it was common courtesy for the host to ensure that the feet of guests were washed after walking the dusty roads. The disciples were embarrassed that they had ignored this common courtesy, and the one they called Teacher and Lord had washed their feet. Jesus affirmed their understanding of His true identity and indicated that they should follow His example and wash each other's feet (vv. 13–14). Jesus' intent was not to establish foot washing as an ordinance such as baptism, but He was teaching that followers of Christ must be servants. This passage is descriptive of an actual event but not prescriptive in the sense that foot washing must be practiced in every church meeting.

HELPFUL HINTS

- Watch for natural divisions in the text.
- Pay attention to the amount of space devoted to a topic.
- Note the repetition of certain words, phrases, or themes.
- Look for relationships in the text.
- Distinguish between matters that are prescriptive and those that are descriptive.

Eight Questions to Ask the Text and Eight to Ask Yourself

What must I ask of the text (often referred to as *exegesis*)?

1. Who wrote this book and what do I know about him?

Gain as much information as possible from the book itself and then consult your commentary or a good Bible dictionary.

2. What were the author's circumstances at the time he was writing?

For example, it may be helpful to know that Paul was traveling on a particular missionary journey or in prison when he wrote a specific book.

3. Who was the original intended audience, and what do I know about them?

Once again, attempt first to answer this by a repeated reading of the book.

4. When was the passage written, and where was the author?

You may need a commentary or a study Bible that includes an introduction to each book to help answer this question.

5. Why was the passage written? Does it have a stated purpose?

6. What was the intent or meaning of a particular text to the original audience? What problems was the author attempting to solve, and what solutions did he offer?

For example, when we read 1 Corinthians 14 we can readily see that unrestrained use of certain spiritual gifts had caused confusion in the gathered assembly. Thus Paul gave specific instructions concerning how many persons may speak and how the abuse of gifts can be controlled.

7. What is the central theme or key verse of each passage?

Finding a key verse will help you remember what a particular chapter or verse is about. For example, the key verse for 1 Corinthians 14 is verse 12. It tells us that the Corinthians were zealous for spiritual gifts and that Paul wanted to redirect that zeal toward gifts that were suited for edifying the assembly.

8. What did the author desire for his audience to do?

WHAT MUST I ASK MYSELF (OFTEN REFERRED TO AS HERMENEUTICS)?

1. *How does this passage apply to my life?*

2. *What did God teach me today?*

3. *Is there a truth I need to apply or a sin I need to avoid?*

4. *How will I apply (obey) these biblical truths today? How does this truth affect my relationship with God and with others?*

5. *Is there a verse I need to memorize?*

6. *What truth or principle should I meditate on today?*

7. *What do I need to record in my notebook today?*

8. *Is there someone with whom I need to share today's lesson?*

DIGGING FOR GOLD IS GREAT FUN, FINDING IT BRINGS GREAT JOY, AND SHARING IT INCREASES ITS IMPACT!

MINE THE GOLD

1. See what characteristics of *historical context* you can find in Amos 1:1.

2. List the two sets of eight questions in your notebook or on the blank pages in your Bible so you will have them readily available.

3. Read the first chapter of 1 Peter and see how many of the eight questions from "What must I ask of the text?" you can answer. Check your answers with Appendix D. Remember: your answers need not be exactly like those in the appendix.

4. In preparation for the next chapter, read Ephesians through five times and see if you can spot an outline emerging.

Digging Deeper: Studying an Entire Book

—✠—

One of the most thorough and rewarding ways to study God's Word is to study an entire book. This method of digging for gold should occupy the majority of your study time. We will look together at some of the key elements in effective book study, and then we will look briefly at the book of Ephesians to provide an example of how a Bible book study should proceed.

STEP 1: CHOOSE YOUR BOOK

The first step is the selection of a book. If this type of study is new to you, I would highly recommend that you choose a book short enough that you can complete it successfully. A number of the Pauline Letters and General Epistles are short enough to qualify in this regard. Once you have completed one successful book study, you will have the confidence to tackle another book. If you study a book like 1 Thessalonians or 1 Peter that has a second volume, it is always a good idea to continue your study until you complete the series. A second suggestion is that you choose a book that already interests you. Your interest may have been spurred by devotional reading or survey reading in that book. Another possibility is that you may choose a book that you are studying in your small group Bible study at church. Sometimes a message your pastor preaches or a verse a friend shares with you will create an interest in a particular book. When the Spirit prompts you to study a particular book, simply follow His direction.

STEP 2: READ THE BOOK MULTIPLE TIMES

Before you begin to ask any specific questions in the attempt to understand an individual chapter or verse, you should read the book several times in a single setting. Set aside enough time that you will be able to read a book repeatedly without being interrupted. You can also alternate between reading a book and listening to it in a recorded format. Sometimes you will hear something as you listen that you didn't notice in your reading. I would also suggest that you read the book from several different translations. You will be amazed at the level of understanding you will achieve simply through the process of multiple readings. You will begin to see the themes that run through the book. You will notice key words and ideas that will enhance your understanding and guide your study. Anytime you read and study the Bible you should have your notebook and pen (or computer if you prefer) handy to record any initial thoughts or questions you might have. Write down any themes or ideas that you want to pursue as you begin more intensive study.

WHENEVER YOU ARE READING OR STUDYING
THE BIBLE, BE PREPARED TO HEAR GOD
SPEAK. HAVE SOMETHING AVAILABLE TO
RECORD THOUGHTS, IDEAS, OR QUESTIONS.

STEP 3: WRITE YOUR OWN INTRODUCTION AND ANSWER KEY QUESTIONS

After your initial reading, see if you can summarize the book in a short paragraph. Can you identify a key theme or key verse? If so, write these in your notebook. You can also begin to answer several of the key questions that we discovered in the last chapter. For example, see if you can answer the following: (1) who wrote the book; (2) what were the author's circumstances at the time of the writing; (3) to whom was it addressed; (4) when was it written; and (5) why was it written. In a broader context you can ask, (6) what did it mean to the original audience; (7) what is the central truth of the book; and (8) what did the author want the readers to do. You can actually put these eight questions on different pages or sections of your notebook and use them as you reread the book. It may take several readings to adequately answer all of these questions, but your "digging" will be well rewarded. Once you have finished answering these questions to the best of your ability, you can compare your findings with those you might find in a commentary or an introduction to the particular book you are studying.

For example, in regards to Ephesians, I believe that verse 3 in the first chapter is a good summary verse: "Blessed be the God and Father of our Lord Jesus Christ, who has blessed us with every spiritual blessing in the heavenly places in Christ." The central idea is that individual believers have been richly blessed by the exalted Christ. We have been joined together into one community that is empowered and commissioned to express God's fullness in the same manner as Christ did during his incarnation.

Now let's address several of the questions that we will pose as we read the book. We find our answer to the questions about authorship and recipients in Ephesians 1:1–2. Paul, who described himself as an apostle, wrote this letter to the saints or believers in Ephesus. There are several references to indicate that Paul wrote this letter from prison. In 3:1 he referred to himself as "the prisoner of Christ Jesus," and in 6:20 he indicated that he was "an ambassador in chains." If we follow the account of Paul's journey from the book of Acts, it seems likely that this letter was written during His Roman imprisonment. The tenor of the book suggests it was intended to encourage the church to live worthy of its high calling and full empowering.

As you read and answer the questions concerning the author, the setting, and the audience, you will unearth unexpected treasures. In this case, we see Paul's love for the church and his passion to see it live up to its potential. That is made even more significant when we understand that he was near the end of his earthly ministry. A similar observation can be made when one reads Philippians, which was also written from a Roman prison. It might surprise you to hear that Philippians is one of the most joyous books of the Bible. That fact helps us to understand that joy is not based on the circumstances of one's life but on one's relationship to Christ.

> AS YOU READ AND ANSWER THE
> QUESTIONS . . . YOU WILL UNEARTH
> UNEXPECTED TREASURES.

As you study an individual book, remember that the answer to some questions may be found in related books. This is particularly true when you are studying one of the

Pauline Letters. You should always read the section or sections in Acts that relate to the community being addressed in a particular letter. Since we are looking at Ephesians together, let me illustrate. You will need to turn to Acts 19–20. In these chapters, we discover that Paul came to Ephesus while Apollos was in Corinth. Upon arriving in Ephesus, he found some disciples who had experienced only John's baptism and were not aware of the work of the Holy Spirit. Further, we note that Paul began his ministry in the synagogue, speaking boldly for three months (19:8). When conflict arose, he continued to meet with the disciples for two years (19:10). Paul's ministry was fortified with miraculous events, which eventually led to a spiritual showdown that caused many who practiced magic to denounce their evil practices and burn their books (19:18–20). This led to a major disturbance created by those who crafted idols because they saw an end to their lucrative business. After the riot was quelled, Paul determined it would be best for him to depart and not to put the church at risk (20:1).

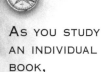

AS YOU STUDY AN INDIVIDUAL BOOK, REMEMBER THAT THE ANSWER TO SOME QUESTIONS MAY BE FOUND IN RELATED BOOKS.

Chapter 20 gives us further details of Paul's travels after his hasty departure from Ephesus. On his return voyage from Macedonia he determined to sail past Ephesus so that he could be in Jerusalem for Pentecost (v. 16). From Miletus, just off the coast of Ephesus, Paul sent for the elders of the church at Ephesus. There are few scenes in Scripture as moving as the reunion with the elders from Ephesus. Paul told them that the Holy Spirit had shown him that chains and afflictions were awaiting him in Jerusalem

(v. 23), and they would never see his face again (v. 25). He charged them to watch out for the church since men from among them would rise up with deviant doctrines to lure the disciples into following them (v. 30). Their affection for Paul was evident as they had a final prayer meeting that ended with much weeping.

This information from Acts tells us much about the church in Ephesus and their respect for their founder. As you read the book of Ephesians you will notice an emphasis on the teaching and leadership gifts (4:11). Paul wanted to undergird the ministry of the authentic leaders so that the younger and more impressionable members would not fall prey to false teachers. Further, the application of the appropriate use of gifts is specifically related to the growth of the church into maturity, which will result in doctrinal stability: "As a result, we are no longer to be children, tossed here and there by waves and carried about by every wind of doctrine, by the trickery of men, by craftiness in deceitful scheming" (4:14). Thus the content of Ephesians is clarified as we read Luke's account of the church in the book of Acts.

STEP 4: WRITE A BRIEF SUMMARY
OF EACH CHAPTER

As you continue your practice of repeated readings, you will find it helpful to write a brief summary of the primary thrust of each chapter. In Ephesians, chapter 1 gives us a brief look at the spiritual blessings. Chapter 2 speaks of the incredible truth that we who were once dead were made alive by Gods' grace, and therefore we have become His workmanship. One aspect of His workmanship is the breaking down of all barrier walls through the cross. Chapter 3 tells us of Paul's unique ministry to the Gentiles and includes a prayer that the church will fully express God's fullness.

Chapter 4 provides a brief look at the unified working of the gifted community that enables the church to express God's fullness. For believers to live in unity we must put off the old man and put on the new man, which results in an edifying, Christian walk. Chapter 5 begins with a continued call to a worthy walk for the believer and ends with a profound declaration of Christ's love for His church by comparing it to marriage. Chapter 6 begins with a look at family relationships and ends with a description of the spiritual armor that will allow us to stand victoriously against the adversary.

In mining for gold, it is important that we first read and understand the overall message of the book because this understanding will help us to interpret individual passages correctly. Understanding the larger context will keep us from mining "fools' gold." Many false interpretations of individual verses are caused by a failure to understand the larger context.

MANY FALSE INTERPRETATIONS OF INDIVIDUAL VERSES ARE CAUSED BY A FAILURE TO UNDERSTAND THE LARGER CONTEXT.

STEP 5: OUTLINE THE BOOK

As you read the book through again, find and mark the major divisions in thought. Once you have identified the major sections, you can see if there are any natural subdivisions within a major section and mark them. Many study Bibles will aid you in this process because they will often indent or mark major sections and give them a heading. Remember that verse and chapter divisions are not original to the text. There is no single, correct way to outline a book, and thus you should trust your own work. Once you have decided upon the major points and sub-points, give each section a brief but descriptive title. This outline will help you to remember what is in a particular book and where it may be found.

The following brief outline of Ephesians will help you to have an understanding of how to proceed. Try your hand at outlining the book by filling in the blanks below.

I. Introduction and Salutation (1:1–3)

II. Every Spiritual Blessing (1:4–14; Reserved for believers in the heavenly places and are available in Christ. List those blessings.)

a. v. 4 _____

b. v. 5–6 _____

c. v. 7 _____

d. vv. 8–10 _____

e. vv. 11–12 _____

f. vv. 13–14 _____

III. A Prayer for Enlightenment (1:15–23; How and what does Paul pray for them?)

a. vv. 15–17 _____

_____

b. vv. 18–23 _____

_____

IV. Alive Together with Christ (2:1–10; Describe the conversion experience.)

a. vv. 1–3 _____

_____

b. vv. 4–7 _____

_____

c. vv. 8–9 _____

_____

d. v. 10 _____

_____

V. He Himself Is Our Peace (2:11–22; Describe our new relationship with God.)

a. vv. 11–12 _____

b. vv. 13–18 _____

c. vv. 19–22 _____

VI. The Mystery Hidden for Ages (3:1–21; How does God make it known to us?)

a. vv. 1–7 _____

b. vv. 8–13 _____

c. vv. 14–21 _____

VII. The Gifted Community Expressing God's Fullness (4:1–16; Picture of a church)

a. vv. 1–3 _____

b. vv. 4–6 _____

c. vv. 7–10 _____

d. vv. 11–12 _____

e. vv. 13–16 _____

VIII. Off with the Old, On with the New (4:17–32; Picture of a new believer)

    a. vv. 17–19 _____

    b. vv. 20–24 _____

    c. vv. 25–32 _____

IX. Follow the Leader (5:1–21; How do we walk as believers?)

    a. vv. 1–2 _____

    b. vv. 3–5 _____

    c. vv. 6–14 _____

    d. vv. 15–21 _____

X. Christ and His Church (5:22–33; How a bride and groom relate to each other)

    a. vv. 22–24 _____

    b. vv. 25–31 _____

    c. vv. 32–33 _____

XI. Family Relationships (6:1–9; How a relationship with Jesus affects all relationships)

    a. vv. 1–3 _____

    b. v. 4 _____

    c. vv. 5–9 _____

XII. Put on the Full Armor of God (6:10–24; Picture of preparing to go into battle)

    a. vv. 10–13 _____

    b. vv. 14–17 _____

    c. vv. 18–20 _____

    d. vv. 21–24 _____

How do you think you did on your outline? If you would like to compare your answers to an outline I completed, see Appendix E. Remember: there is no single, correct way to outline a book.

Use your outline during your more detailed study of individual passages to help you keep the whole message of the book in view. This will assist you in connecting the individual passages and truths you learn to the central message of the book.

STEP 6: STUDY EACH VERSE IN ITS CONTEXT

The first task is to determine the exact meaning of each word in each verse in the context in which it is found. You will need to look first at the words in each verse and determine their meanings. You will want to do your own study before consulting a Bible dictionary. Many of the words will be quite familiar, and their meaning in the sentence will be obvious. Others may require additional study. For example, the word "fullness" in Ephesians 1:23 is a word that may cause you to ponder its actual meaning.

The best way to determine the meaning of a word is to study its usage in the Bible itself and, in particular, in the book you are studying, along with any other writings by that same author. You may recall that we looked at the uniqueness of the word "fullness" in the Ephesian letter in the last chapter. The term first occurs in 1:10 where Paul spoke of "the fullness of the times." The meaning in that context is made perfectly clear as Paul was speaking of the end of time when God will sum up everything in Christ. The meaning here is similar to the usage in Galatians 4:4 where God sent His Son to earth in "the fullness of the time." The incarnation occurred at precisely the time God intended, and the return of Jesus will occur on God's precise timetable.

The meaning of "fullness" in 1:23 must be slightly different since the verse speaks of the church as "the fullness of Him who fills all in all." Reading in context, we discover that the church is the fullness of God by virtue of the resurrection and glorious ascension of Christ (1:18–22). As we

 continue to look for this particular word, we will find it again in 3:19. Here Paul prayed

THE CHURCH IS THE FULLNESS OF GOD BY . . . THE RESURRECTION AND ASCENSION.

that his readers would experience inner strength and know the love of Christ so that they "may be filled up to all the fullness of God." This usage is consistent with 1:23 and declares that the church can attain the fullness for which it was designed by God as its individual members embrace all that God has prepared for them. A final usage is found in 4:13 where Paul discussed the results of the gifted community working together. As gifted leaders help members to discover and develop their gifts, the church will attain to unity and maturity which is measured by "the stature which belongs to the fullness of Christ." It is apparent that we are mining pure gold as we follow this vein in Paul's thought. The church is no ordinary community! It is *extraordinary* in that it is empowered and commissioned to express God's fullness.

But this vein of gold goes deeper. We can trace the vein further if we remember that Paul wrote Ephesians and Colossians at the same time. Thus we turn to Colossians 1:19 and discover this great declaration: "For it was the Father's good pleasure for all the fullness to dwell in Him." Now put these two ideas together. It was God's desire to express His fullness in Christ during the time of His incarnation. It is now His plan to express His fullness through the church. We must never underestimate the work of the church.

Once you have determined the meaning of individual words, notice the context in which they occur—what goes before and what comes after. R. A. Torrey illustrated the importance of this principle by looking at John 14:18:"I will not leave you as orphans; I will come to you." The question raised by this text is what Jesus meant by the promise, "I will come to you." Three different answers have been suggested: the postresurrection appearances, the second coming, or His coming through the gift of the Spirit. If such disagreement exists among scholars, is it possible for a lay student to know what is meant? Take a moment and read this verse in its context. Verses 16–17 and verses 25–26 both speak of the ministry of the Spirit. John was talking about the ministry of the Holy Spirit that would soon be available to all believers. The question is easily resolved by attention to the context.[1] Word study that pays clear attention to context will yield rich gold.

STEP 7: ANALYZE EACH VERSE BY ASKING WHAT IT TEACHES

Having determined the meaning of the verse in its context, you should then analyze the verse by asking what it teaches. Don't assume you have finished this task by your first response. As you come to a verse again and again, new truths will begin to present themselves. As they do, write them down in your notebook.

Let's analyze a familiar verse as an example of this process. No doubt you have committed John 3:16 to memory, so let's analyze it:

1. God is the subject of the sentence and the author of all that follows.

2. The activity described in the verse is prompted by God's love. God's nature is to love.

3. The object of His love is everyone in the world. His love is unlimited in its scope.

4. His love prompted a tangible and sacrificial action—"He gave." The atonement was not an action forced upon God, but one which He voluntarily gave.

5. The gift of God was His "only begotten Son." His Son was unique and thus the only one qualified to save man.

6. "Whoever" means His death was sufficient for all.

7. To appropriate the saving grace of God found in the gift of His Son, man must believe "in Him."

8. Those who believe in Him "shall not perish but have eternal life."

God's truth is so inexhaustible that our list of eight observations only scratches the surface of this great verse. Perhaps you thought of others as you read the above paragraph and meditated on John 3:16. We could come back to this verse time and again and find something we did not see before. The gold we find in God's Word is inexhaustible.

STEP 8: CLASSIFY YOUR RESULTS

Once you complete a book through verse-by-verse study, you will want to look back over your notes and attempt to classify your results. This step of classification will allow you to have your notes in an orderly shape which will enable you to find verses, truths, and themes in the future and share them with others. You can begin by making a complete list of the subjects you discovered in a particular book along with the biblical references that comment on the subject. How you go about organizing your material will depend upon the book studied and your own particular interest. Most books will cover subjects such as God, Jesus Christ, the Holy Spirit, the believer, the church, salvation, the world, the Word of God, ethical behavior, and many other related topics. Many of these topics may have obvious subtopics. For example, in Ephesians the topics of God and the church will have numerous references that could well be divided into many subdivisions. Take your time and enjoy the mining process; you will discover rich veins of gold.

STEP 9: MEDITATE, MEMORIZE, AND RESPOND

The final step should never be overlooked. We must meditate upon the results of our study and determine what we must do to respond to God's Word. While mining for gold in God's Word is fun and stimulating, our purpose is to know God better by responding fully to His Word. Remember: "All Scripture is inspired by God and profitable for teaching, for reproof, for correction, for training in righteousness" (2 Tim. 3:16). Remind yourself of the eight questions we must ask of each text. These eight questions will guide your time of meditation. As you ponder the wonderful truths you have discovered, ask the Holy Spirit to illuminate them and help you to apply them. As you meditate upon the incredible truths you have discovered through book study, begin to memorize key verses in the book. These memorized verses will continually minister to you and allow you to minister to others. They will help you to remember your outline of the book and where you found certain truths. You should also seek opportunities to share truths you have learned with others.

MINE THE GOLD

1. Answer these questions:

   a. How did your outline of Ephesians compare with the one in Appendix E?

   b. What truths from Ephesians most impacted your life?

   c. What verses from Ephesians do you desire to commit to memory?

   d. Are you working faithfully to develop a notebook for Bible study?

2. Write verses to memorize on a 3 by 5 card. Put the verse and its reference on one side and the topic on the other.

Discovering Gold in Topical Studies

Most of your digging for gold will likely take place as you mine the veins you discover through the study of individual books. However, you will frequently find that while you are studying a book or participating in a small group Bible study through your church, a particular topic may occupy your mind continually, and you will want to keep excavating a particular vein of gold you have uncovered. Topical studies add depth and interest to your regular study of individual books and provide unique insights into the truths contained in Scripture.

There are several ways of going about topical studies, and thus you should let your desire, informed by the Holy Spirit, be your guide. For example, you may find that you are interested in a particular topic such as the family, grace, love, faith, or prayer. You can joyfully follow the desire the Holy Spirit has birthed in you. One topical approach is to look at various doctrines such as the doctrine of God, the Holy Spirit, the atonement, the second coming, or heaven. Another variation in the topical approach to study is to look at Old or New Testament characters or the women of the Bible. The topical approach is only limited by your own Spirit-informed imagination.

You may find it possible to do a topical study while you are still participating in your daily book study, or you may take a break from your book study to follow a topic at the Spirit's prompting.

There are a few words of caution that we need to consider. It is easy to get so focused on a single topic that you can get bogged down and fail to get a balanced diet of God's Word. I have known people who became so intrigued with numerology (the study of numbers) or the doctrine of the second coming of Christ that they became one-sided and failed to develop a well-rounded understanding of the Bible.

ANTICIPATE THE SPIRIT'S GUIDANCE WHEN SELECTING TOPICS

The more you study the Bible, the more you will want to study it. Maybe your digging for gold in God's Word began as a sense of duty, but you soon discovered that it has become your passion. The more you study, the more your appetite for God's Word will grow. You can rely on the Holy Spirit to both guide you in your study and to help you understand what you study. Be careful! As we become more adept at Bible study, we can be tempted to become too reliant upon our methods of study and lose our attentiveness to the Spirit who authored the book. Listen to His voice; He inspired the authors who wrote Scripture, and He will inform your mind as you plan your study.

CLAIM THIS PROMISE:

"BUT THE HELPER, THE HOLY SPIRIT, WHOM THE FATHER WILL SEND IN MY NAME, HE WILL TEACH YOU ALL THINGS, AND BRING TO YOUR REMEMBRANCE ALL THAT I SAID TO YOU." (JOHN 14:26)

Often when you are involved in a book study, you will find yourself thinking, "I would love to have more time to devote to this topic." You don't want to get distracted and lose the focus of your book study. What should you do? When that occurs, jot your idea down on a page in your notebook devoted to "topics to study." I have learned that I can't simply rely on my memory. It helps to keep a list of studies I desire to pursue. On other occasions, I find that topics of interest are triggered by a message I have heard, a book I am reading, or the circumstances of my life. For example, if you are ministering to someone with a terminal illness, you may find yourself drawn to a topical study of heaven. What you learn during this topical study will help you to minister to your friend or loved one while at the same time you are finding great nuggets of truth for your own edification.

BE WELL-ROUNDED IN YOUR TOPICAL STUDY

As you are making your list of the various subjects you would like to study, think about a logical order for moving from topic to topic. For example, if you were interested in topics related to systematic theology (the systematic study of God), you could begin by listing major categories such as God, Jesus Christ, Holy Spirit, Trinity, creation, man, fall, sin, redemption, virgin birth, incarnation, the cross, the resurrection, the second coming, heaven, hell, and so on. Most of these topics can be further subdivided. For example, if you wanted to study the doctrine of Jesus Christ, you could look at His divinity, human nature, death, resurrection, ascension, return, and present and future reigns. You could also look at the different titles or names used for Jesus.

GOD'S WORD HAS COUNTLESS VEINS OF GOLD.

Another area that lends itself to topical study is biographical study. In this case you would choose a person or group of persons that interest you. For example Luke 8:2 mentions "some women." He then names some of these women in verses 2–3. Who were these women, and why did Luke include them are questions that a topical study will answer.

You could also take the twelve disciples, the patriarchs, the kings of the south, or the judges as groups of persons you want to study. The options are endless. Truly God's Word has countless veins of gold.

Any time you study a person, you will want to find all the references to this person in the entire Bible. Once again a good concordance is an indispensable tool (see Appendix B). As you study a character make sure you read the entire section where he or she is mentioned. You can approach a biographical study from various angles: the person's character, strengths and weaknesses, mistakes made, accomplishments in life, difficulties he or she overcame, and successes and failures. For example, Sampson the judge makes for a fascinating study. He had great potential, and yet he had glaring weaknesses that often handicapped him in his work. Daniel and his three friends are great prospects for a topical study about how to thrive in a hostile environment. In the study of Daniel, you can actually combine a topical study with a book study. When doing a topical study on a person or persons, make a sketch of the person's life. For example, Paul was a persecutor of the church who was saved through a dramatic encounter with the resurrected Lord. He subsequently became one of the great missionaries of all time and the author of twelve New Testament letters. Summarize the lessons we can learn from each person.

You will find it helpful to dedicate an entire notebook to your topical studies. In due time, you will probably have several notebooks filled with topical studies. You could put your list of topics to study in the front of each notebook and then establish tabs for each topic as you complete a study. Having a comprehensive topical notebook will help to ensure that you are being well-rounded in your study. It will also help you to see how many of these topics intersect at various places as you continue to mine for gold.

Be Thorough

God's Word is too precious for us to study in a haphazard manner. You will want to cover all the passages which deal with a particular topic, and these can be found in your concordance. Remember: you will need a concordance that is keyed to the translation you use for Bible study. You will want to list and look up every passage that has the key word for your topic of interest. Most good concordances will list the word in a phrase so you can read the phrase and determine whether a particular usage relates to your specific interest before you take the time to look it up in its original context. This is especially helpful when you choose a word or phrase that is used a large number of times. Looking up several hundred references can be a bit daunting. I would generally recommend that you choose a topic without a vast number of references for your first venture into topical study.

The study of a topic will often require you to look up related words, which will enable you to develop a thorough understanding of a particular topic. Let's say that we wanted to study the topic of prayer so we could develop a more effective prayer life. What words would you look up? You would obviously begin with the word *pray* and various cognates such as *prayed, prayers, praying,* and *prays.* But the vein of gold is so deep here, you should think about related words such as *ask, petition, intercession, call upon, seek, knock, praise,* and so on. Many of these words will occur to you as you begin to read the different verses on prayer that you find in your concordance. You will often find that each topical study will be an open-ended study. In other words, when you are doing devotional or study reading, you may unearth new and unexpected verses on a topic you studied in the past. The same would be true for a book. When you find such a gold nugget, go back and add it to your original notes on the topic or Bible book.

If you purchase a computer-aided Bible study program, an excellent concordance may be included, or one can be unlocked and added to the tools that are included with your program. One of the advantages of the computer version of the concordance is the speed with which you can do a word or topical search. A further advantage is that you can give additional specifications for any search, which can enable you to do a much more targeted search. You can have your computer search for a word used in a specific phrase or combination of words. For example, searching for "love and hope" together will yield a smaller sample than looking for each word individually.

Various topical Bibles and books will arrange passages of Scripture by subjects. These may provide a jump start for your study, but don't rely on them alone. Do your own digging. You never know what you will find when you truly seek.

BE PRECISE IN YOUR STUDY METHODOLOGY

A topical study must be undertaken with the same discipline and diligence you would use in your verse-by-verse study. In other words, you are not simply listing verses on a particular topic. You want to make sure that you are reading each verse in light of its context. You will want to read the entire passage and not just the single verse mentioned in the concordance. It is important that you ask the two sets of eight key questions we discovered in chapter 4, questions that you should ask of any verse that you study. The gold you will uncover is priceless, and your efforts to unearth pure gold must be diligent.

As you list a verse in your topical notebook, record all of your insights from the context and the various questions you asked of the text. When your study is this precise and thorough, you will be able to refer to it at any time in the future and remind yourself of the insights you gained through your original study. This will prove invaluable when you need to share the results of your study with someone in the future. God wastes nothing! Every gold nugget you find will prove to be of great value time and again.

CLASSIFY AND WRITE DOWN YOUR RESULTS

We have already mentioned the need to keep good records of our discoveries, but I can't emphasize this often enough. Have you ever lost something that was precious to you? Of course you have! When this occurs, we spend countless hours searching for an item that we are certain we once possessed. It is frustrating and time-consuming. It is always better to take a little extra time at the outset and create a system that will enable us to have immediate access to every gold nugget we have found.

No one can tell you how to organize your own material, but it must be organized so that it is readily available to you. Look for a system that makes sense to you and then create a cross-reference guide. For example, when I was actively pastoring a church, I would file my messages by topic, date preached, and by Scripture reference. When I wanted to locate a particular message, I had several different ways to aid me in finding the message I wanted. Nobody wants to discover gold and then forget where they found it or stored it!

I would also suggest that you leave several pages blank at the end of each topic in your notebook. You will find that your ongoing book and topical study will allow you to unearth new nuggets that you will want to add to your original and ongoing study of a topic. God's Word is so vast, and the treasures it contains are so incredible that you will find it impossible to exhaust the gold discovered in any one vein that you uncover.

Enjoy Discovering God's Gold

So I will ask again the question I posed in chapter 1: What if you discovered there was a vein of gold in your backyard? How would you respond? What would you do to discover the extent of the gold you now own and then obtain it? I suspect you would not waste any time before you began digging for the gold. I also imagine that you would spare no expense purchasing the tools you needed to unearth it. Then you would work tirelessly and joyfully to fully possess it. God's Word contains inexhaustible riches that will provide abundant joy in this life and treasure in heaven. As you begin, continue, or improve your Bible study practices through what you have learned in this book, I want you to enjoy the journey with God.

> The law of the LORD is perfect, restoring the soul;
> The testimony of the LORD is sure, making wise
>   the simple.
> The precepts of the LORD are right, rejoicing the heart;
> The commandment of the LORD is pure,
>   enlightening the eyes.
> The fear of the LORD is clean, enduring forever;
> The judgments of the LORD are true; they are righteous
>   altogether.
> They are more desirable than gold, yes, than much
>   fine gold;
> Sweeter also than honey and the drippings of the
>   honeycomb.
>
> (Ps. 19:7–10)

MINE THE GOLD

I know that it is unusual to give an assignment at the end of a study, but I am praying that this final chapter doesn't mark the end of a study but the beginning of a lifelong quest for pure gold.

1. Memorize Psalm 19:7–10.

2. Review and rehearse the books of the Bible, making sure you have them clear in your mind.

3. Purchase several notebooks in anticipation of your gold-digging future. You can also create files on your computer and maintain your files in Google Docs or the iCloud at no charge. This will allow you to access your files from any computer.

4. Begin a topical study on "the inspiration of the Bible."

5. Make this commitment: With God's help I will embark on a lifelong adventure to discover the pure gold contained in His Word. I covenant to read God's Word daily, to be faithful in corporate and personal Bible study, to develop a plan of study and memorization, and to respond to the Word under the direction of the Holy Spirit.

Signed _____

Date _____

Appendix A

HOW TO BEGIN A RELATIONSHIP WITH CHRIST

Everyone desires a full and meaningful life, and God wants you to experience life to its fullest and to live eternally with Him. God gave the Bible to us so that we might know Him in a personal relationship. Beginning a relationship with Christ requires a simple commitment, and that will lead to a lifelong journey that grows in depth. I use a simple acrostic—LIFE—to help people begin this journey.

L = Love

It all begins with God's love. God created you in His image, which means that you are relational, rational, and responsible. He wants you to live in relationship with Him, and thus He has revealed Himself in history, which is recorded in the Bible. John's gospel says, "For God so loved the world, that He gave His only begotten Son, that whoever believes in Him shall not perish, but have eternal life" (3:16). If God loves you and desires a relationship with you, why do you feel so isolated from Him?

I = Isolation

Our isolation was caused by our sin—our rebellion against God—which separates us from Him since he is holy: "For all have sinned and fall short of the glory of God. For the wages of sin is death, but the free gift of God is eternal life in Christ Jesus our Lord" (Rom. 3:23; 6:23). "Death" refers to our spiritual death and consequent separation from God. Perhaps you are wondering how you can overcome this isolation and have an intimate and eternal relationship with God.

F = *Forgiveness*

The only solution to a human's isolation and separation from a holy God is forgiveness: "If we say that we have no sin, we are deceiving ourselves and the truth is not in us. If we confess our sins, He is faithful and righteous to forgive us our sins and to cleanse us from all unrighteousness" (1 John 1:8–9). To confess our sin, we must first agree with God about our condition and then desire to turn away from our sin and turn to Him.

The only way we can have a relationship with a holy God is through the forgiveness of our sin. The sinless Son of God died on the cross to forgive your sin. He paid the penalty for you.

E = *Eternal Life*

You can have a full and abundant life now and eternal life when you die. Jesus said, "I came that they may have life, and have it abundantly. This is eternal life, that they may know You, the only true God, and Jesus Christ whom You have sent" (John 10:10b; 17:3). Can you think of any reason you wouldn't like to have a personal relationship with God? Beginning that relationship is as easy as **ABC**:

> **A** = **Admit** you are a sinner. Turn from your sin and turn to God: "Therefore repent and return, so that your sins may be wiped away, in order that times of refreshing may come from the presence of the Lord" (Acts 3:19).

B = **Believe** that Jesus died for your sins and rose from the dead to enable you to have eternal life: "These things I have written to you who believe in the name of the Son of God, so that you may know that you have eternal life" (1 John 5:13).

C = **Confess** your commitment to Jesus as Lord of your life verbally and publicly: "That if you confess with your mouth Jesus as Lord, and believe in your heart that God has raised Him from the dead, you will be saved" (Rom. 10:9).

You must first confess these truths to God. You can invite Jesus Christ to be your Lord and Savior right now. Confess to Him something like this, but feel free to put it in your own words.

> God, I admit that I am a sinner. I turn from my sin and I turn to you. I believe that you sent Jesus, who died on the cross and rose from the dead, paying the penalty for my sins. I ask you to forgive my sin and I gladly receive your gift of eternal life. In Jesus name, I ask for this gift. Amen.

If you have a friend or family member who is a Christian, tell that person about your decision. Then find a church that believes and teaches the Bible, and let the people there help you grow deeper in your relationship with Christ. To remind you of this commitment, why not sign and date this page?

Signed _____

Date _____

Appendix B

Study Bible

Your first essential tool is a study Bible in the translation of your preference. A study Bible will often include maps, outlines, introductions to books, and other helpful resources. Your Christian bookstore manager can help you find an appropriate study Bible. There are also chain-reference Bibles and topical study Bibles that will help you, particularly in thematic and topical studies. Two helpful study Bibles are:

- Thompson Chain Reference Bible
- Nave's Topical Bible

Bible Dictionary

A Bible dictionary will not only help you define certain terms but will provide other essential background material. Some good dictionaries include:

- *Eerdman's Dictionary of the Bible*
- *Nelson's Illustrated Bible Dictionary, New and Enhanced Edition*
- *NIV Compact Dictionary of the Bible*
- *Tyndale Bible Dictionary*
- *W. E. Vine's New Testament Word Pictures, Matthew to Acts*
- *W.E. Vine's New Testament Word Pictures, Romans to Revelation*

Bible Handbook

A Bible handbook combines a Bible dictionary and commentary. Here are some options:

- *Halley's Bible Handbook*
- *The New Unger's Bible Handbook*

Bible Concordance

A concordance will assist you in word studies since it will list other occurrences of a particular word. You may want to purchase a compact concordance. An exhaustive concordance will contain a more extensive list of entries. The most popular concordance may be Strong's, but you want to make sure you choose a concordance that is keyed to the Bible translation of your choice.

Bible Atlas

A Bible Atlas includes not only detailed Bible maps, it also contains important articles that will help you understand the geography and topography of the Bible lands. Some popular choices are:

- *Holman Bible Atlas*
- *Zondervan Atlas of the Bible*

Bible Software Programs

Bible software programs include numerous resources to assist in Bible study including maps, dictionaries, multiple translations, commentaries, and dictionaries. Most will come with a basic library and will allow the user to unlock various tools for reasonable prices. You can build a complete Bible library rather inexpensively in this manner. The other advantage of software libraries is the speed of the search using any software program. You might want to consider:

- Accordance Bible Software
- Logos Bible Software
- Olive Tree Bible Software

Free Online and App Resources

Many tools to help with Bible reading and Bible memorization are free as downloadable apps for a smartphone, iPad, or android device. Here are a few suggestions:

- Bible Gateway . . . . Biblegateway.com
- Bible.cloud
- Bible.is
- Mantis Bible Study . . . . . Mantisbible.com
- Olive Tree Bible . . . . Olivetree.com
- Precept Austin . . . . Preceptaustin.org
- YouVersion . . . . YouVersion.com

Appendix C

Reading Plans

Bible Gateway Reading Plans

https://www.biblegateway.com/reading-plans/

The Moody Church Three-year Bible Reading Plan

http://www.moodychurch.org/static/uploads/globaladmin/
bible_reading_plans/bible_threeyear.pdf

3 Year Bible Reading Plan

http://www.3yearbible.com/wp-content/uploads/2016/01/
3-Year-Bible-Reading-Plan-1.3.pdf

Bible Study Tools Reading Plan

http://www.biblestudytools.com/bible-reading-plan/

Appendix D

1 Peter: What Must I Ask of the Text?

1. Who wrote this book and what do I know about him?
Verse 1 indicates that Peter, who served as an apostle of Jesus Christ, was the author. Fortunately we know a great deal about Peter from the Gospels and Acts. He seems to have been the leader and spokesman for the twelve apostles and was a preeminent missionary to the Gentiles.

2. What were the author's circumstances at the time he was writing?
Chapter 1 does not give us any indication of his personal circumstances.

3. Who was the original intended audience, and what do I know about them?
According to verse 1, Peter sent this letter to "those who reside as aliens, scattered throughout Pontus, Galatia, Cappadocia, Asia, and Bithynia, who are chosen." The term "chosen" indicates he was addressing believers, and the words "aliens" and "scattered" suggests they were suffering from some form of persecution.

4. When was the passage written, and where was the author?
Chapter 1 does not say specifically when it was written or where the author might have been at the time.

5. Why was the passage written? Does it have a stated purpose?
The passage was written to encourage believers who are suffering "various trials" (v. 6) and assure them that their temporary suffering will "result in praise

and glory and honor at the revelation of Jesus Christ"
(v. 7).

6. **What was the intent or meaning of a particular text
to the original audience? What problems was the
author attempting to solve, and what solutions did
he offer?**

The original audience would have been greatly encouraged and fortified by the understanding of their sure
salvation.

7. **What is the central theme or key verse of each
passage?**

In this case the key verse is actually three verses which
is a single sentence (vv. 3–5).

8. **What did the author desire for his audience to do?**

Peter wanted them to keep their focus on the glorious
truth of their salvation so they could be fully assured
and encouraged in the time of their testing. This would
lead them to prepare their minds for action and live holy
lives (vv. 13–16).

Remember: your answers need not be exactly like those
above. Other details about the author and his condition at
the time of the writing are revealed in 5:12–13.

Appendix E

V. He Himself Is Our Peace (2:11–22)

    a. Once excluded (vv. 11–12)

    b. Now one in Christ (vv. 13–18)

    c. We are God's household (vv. 19–22)

VI. The Mystery Hidden for Ages (3:1–21)

    a. According to the grace given to me (vv. 1–7)

    b. The manifold wisdom of God through the church (vv. 8–13)

    c. Beyond all we ask or think through the church (vv. 14–21)

VII. The Gifted Community Expressing God's Fullness (4:1–16)

    a. The worthy walk (vv. 1–3)

    b. Unity, the foundation for gifted ministry (vv. 4–6)

    c. The triumphant King gifts His church (vv. 7–10)

    d. Gifted leaders equipping gifted members (vv. 11–12)

    e. The results of gifted ministry (vv. 13–16)

VIII. Off with the Old, On with the New (4:17–32)

    a. No longer walk in futility (vv. 17–19)

    b. Take off and put on (vv. 20–24)

    c. Members of one another (vv. 25–32)

IX. Follow the Leader (5:1–21)

    a. Walk in love (vv. 1–2)

    b. Walk in purity (vv. 3–5)

    c. Walk as children of light (vv. 6–14)

    d. Walk in wisdom (vv. 15–21)

X. Christ and His Church (5:22–33)

    a. The submission of the bride (vv. 22–24)

    b. The sacrificial love of the husband (vv. 25–31)

    c. The great mystery (5:32–33)

XI. Family Relationships (6:1–9)

    a. Children, obey your parents (vv. 1–3)

    b. Parents, discipline your children (v. 4)

    c. Workers and masters (vv. 5–9)

XII. Put on the Full Armor of God (6:10–24)

    a. A call to arms (vv. 10–13)

    b. The armor described (vv. 14–17)

    c. Covered with prayer (vv. 18–20)

    d. Final thoughts and a benediction (vv. 21–24)

Notes

Chapter 1

1. R. A. Torrey, *How to Study the Bible for Greatest Profit* (Chicago: Fleming H. Revell, 1896), 96. I have profited greatly from the reading of Dr. Torrey's book and have borrowed generously from him in this section.

2. Ibid, 112.

Chapter 2

1. Vaughn Roberts, *God's Big Picture: Tracing the Storyline of the Bible* (Downers Grove, IL: InterVarsity Press, 2002).

Chapter 3

1. Tim LaHaye, *How to Study the Bible for Yourself* (Oregon: Harvest House Publishers, 1976), 44.

2. George H. Guthrie, *Read the Bible for LIFE: Workbook* (Nashville: Lifeway Press, 2010), 29. This entire section is a brief synopsis of much of Guthrie's nine-week study. I highly recommend that study for those who want to get a better understanding of reading in context. It will provide you with an opportunity to practice the reading methods described.

3. Andreas Kostenberger as referenced in George H. Guthrie, *Read the Bible for Life* (Nashville: B&H Publishing, 2010), 43.

4. Guthrie, *Read the Bible for LIFE: Workbook*, 77.

5. Gordon D. Fee & Douglas Stuart, *How to Read the Bible for All Its Worth* (Grand Rapids, Zondervan Publishing House, 1982), 203.

6. Guthrie, 149.

7. Craig Blomberg as referenced in Guthrie, 149.

Chapter 4

1. Gordon D. Fee & Douglas Stuart, *How to Read the Bible for All Its Worth* (Grand Rapids: Zondervan, 1982), 19.

Chapter 5

1. R.A. Torrey, *How To Study the Bible for Greatest Profit* (New York; Fleming H. Revell, 1896), 25f. I have relied heavily on R. A. Torrey's section on the study of individual books throughout this section. This classic is out of print, but you may be able to find a copy from a secondhand book shop.

IF YOU HAVE ENJOYED THIS STUDY FROM KEN HEMPHILL, LOOK FOR THESE OTHER TITLES:

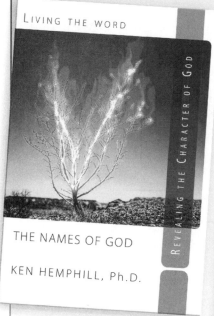

LIVING THE WORD

THE NAMES OF GOD

KEN HEMPHILL, Ph.D.

REVEALING THE CHARACTER OF GOD

NEW TESTAMENT

EVERY SPIRITUAL BLESSING

Ken Hemphill

A STUDY OF EPHESIANS

For these and other small group studies, visit Auxano Press at Auxanopress.com.

Auxano
PRESS